Applying the Children Act (1989) in Boarding and Residential Environments

Dedication

To the Royal Hospital School, Holbrook

Applying the Children Act (1989) in Boarding and Residential Environments

Ewan W. Anderson
and
Alan J. Davison

David Fulton Publishers
London

David Fulton Publishers Ltd
2 Barbon Close, London WC1N 3JX

First published in Great Britain by
David Fulton Publishers 1993

Note: The right of the contributors to be identified as the authors of their work
has been asserted by them in accordance with the Copyright, Designs and
Patents Act 1988.

Copyright © David Fulton (Publishers) Ltd

British Library Cataloguing in Publication Data

A catalogue record for this book is available from the British Library

ISBN 1-85346-257-8

Typeset by Action Typesetting Limited, Gloucester
Printed in Great Britain by The Cromwell Press Ltd, Melksham, Wilts.

Contents

Contributors

Ewan Anderson is Senior Lecturer in Durham University, Boarding Adviser to the Boarding Schools Association and a member of the Wagner Development Working Group. He was responsible for the pilot studies in boarding schools for the implementation of the Children Act

Martin Callow is a former Housemaster at the Royal Hospital School

Norman Cooke is a Senior Teacher at Cloughside School and Psychiatric Centre

Alan Davison is Principal of the Brandon Children's Centre and Chair of the Durham Adoption Panel

Brian FitzGerald is the HMI with special responsibility for boarding and the Children Act

Suzanne Hutchinson is a Housemistress at Ellesmere College

Barbara Kahan is Chair of the National Children's Bureau

Christopher King is a Housemaster at Rendcomb College

David Robinson is a Housemaster at Bootham School

Peter Stone is the SSI with special responsibility for the Children Act

Foreword

Foreword

The Holbrook Group is probably the only active research team which draws its expertise from both boarding and residential education and care, and includes academics, practitioners and central government inspectors. The Group meets regularly in a variety of residential establishments, to discuss problems with the staff and to produce its own material. This volume, concerned specifically with the implementation of the *CHILDREN ACT 1989* summarises much of the Group's current thinking.

In many parts of the world, but particularly in Western Europe, social educators, people who educate children while living with them, are recognised as constituting a distinctive profession. Britain is an exception and those who live with and care for children living in groups away from home, have often been given lower status than the teachers, social workers, psychotherapists and nurses with whom they work. It is hoped that this book may contribute to achieving higher status for those in group care and social education in Britain.

The book identifies many of the key issues which arise in caring for children away from home. These issues are examined, using the framework of the Children Act and its implementation. The concerns analysed and the questions addressed are essentially practical. However, given the broad sweep of the subject, the book is likely to be of interest to many others than practitioners involved in educating or caring for children.

All my own experience has demonstrated the importance of training in this field. Recent experiences, including the Pindown Inquiry and the work of the National Children's Bureau, have further highlighted the particular importance of training not just for practitioners, but for managers at all levels in social services and education departments. I hope that this lively and interesting contribution to the current debate about the care and education of children and young people will be widely read amongst those concerned in many ways with these services.

Barbara Kahan OBE MA(Cantab) MA(OU)

Abbreviations

ACPC	Area Child Protection Committee
BMA	British Medical Association
BSA	Boarding Schools Association
CCETSW	Central Council for Education and Training in Social Work
CHE	Community Home with Education
CLEA	Council of Local Education Authorities
DES	Department of Education and Science
DFE	Department for Education
DH	Department of Health
FICE	Federation Internationale des Communutes Educatives
HMC	Head Masters' Conference
HMI	Her Majesty's Inspector
INSET	In Service Education and Training
ISIS	Independent Schools' Information Service
LASSD	Local Authority Social Services Department
LEA	Local Education Authority
MTP	Measurement of Treatment Potential
NCVCCO	National Council of Voluntary Child Care Organizations
NOC	Notice of Complaint
OED	Oxford English Dictionary
ORD	an Objective, a Relevance to the child, and a Deceleration of problems
PSHE	personal, social and health education
RIBA	Royal Institute of British Architects
SSD	Social Services Department
SSI	Social Services Inspector
UCCA	Universities Central Council on Admissions
URES	University Residence Environment Scale

CHAPTER 1

The Children Act 1989 and Boarding: Background to the Act and the Key Sections

Peter Stone SSI

The boarding school as the setting of choice for educating some children has a hallowed, if sometimes disputed, place in the story of schooling in Great Britain. The image which the name most readily conjures is that of the public school of high social standing, steeped in history and tradition, providing schooling for a minority of children and striving after standards of academic and sporting excellence.

In reality, the sector is much more diverse than this limited stereotype. It includes schools maintained from public funds as well as private ones, large and small, specialist and generalist, those that are well endowed financially and some that struggle to meet high standards while charging affordable fees. Children of all kinds attend them, from many countries and for many reasons. There are almost 1,000 boarding schools in the private sector and about 80 or so provided by local education authorities.

The Children Act 1989 sets out to provide 'a new framework for the care and upbringing of all children'. Those spending part of their childhood lives in boarding schools are not excluded from this, although the Bill originally presented to parliament contained only one proposal of specific relevance to them. This was for the registration of some smaller schools as children's homes, though in the event, the number of schools included within this provision (around 250 or so) proved to be much bigger than initially expected.

The course of the Bill, however, was dramatically affected by revelations in 1989 about events at Crookham Court, a privately owned boarding school in Berkshire. The full story of the school has now passed into history but its main bones bear repeating.

Knowledge and concern about the nature and extent of the abuse of some children had grown throughout the 1970s and 1980s. In the late 1980s the level of concern about the many forms which abuse could take had gained new levels; the child care world and the public had been rocked by the Cleveland cases in 1987; these and others showed the need to make sure that abused children were reliably identified and then properly protected and cared for.

At Crookham Court it had been found that boys had suffered sustained and brutal physical and sexual abuse over many years by the school's proprietor and two other teachers. The case had, justifiably, great prominence in the media, and the TV programme *That's Life* did much to ensure that the public was aware of the issues which the case raised about the well-being of children in residential schools where parents had little contact and where there was no public oversight of their welfare. The Children Bill was before the House of Commons at the time and the level of anxiety in parliament was also very high.

In consequence, a further provision was inserted into the Bill which placed a new legal duty of boarding schools to 'promote and safeguard the welfare' of the pupils they accommodated. This was the same phrase which informed the approach of the whole Bill towards welfare. It also required that Social Services Departments (SSDs) should take all reasonably practicable steps to ensure that the new duty was being adequately discharged. Both this requirement and the earlier registration provisions (which became sections 87 and 63 of the Children Act, respectively) were dramatically new departures for the regulation of boarding schools. I will discuss the main features of both sections later in the chapter.

A special and unusual feature of the development of the Children Act was the extent to which practitioners, academics and government officials worked together in drafting the Bill on which it was based. Its provisions were based on a coherent set of principles which could apply to the position of all children and it arranged for all of them to be treated in the same way before the law, according to the underlying principles and whatever the source of their problems.

The Children Act 1989 which resulted incorporated these principles and its implementation has been marked by a sustained effort to explain them to practitioners in the social welfare and legal fields.

The boarding schools' provisions were no exceptions to this process. HMI and SSI put considerable effort into a development programme of pilot inspections which explored the processes, relationships and practical issues involved in satisfying SSDs about the welfare of children in boarding schools. The lessons of these exercises were disseminated through a seminar programme to practitioners in schools and the child welfare field. A practical guide,[1] and a training pack[2] were published and a survey of the views of 1,500 school pupils about standards is expected shortly.[3] Some of the key messages from these publications are discussed below.

To return, for the moment, to the legislation, the Children Act 1989 was implemented on 14th October 1991. Section 63, together with lengthy associated regulations and guidance,[4] proved controversial and difficult to apply to the schools affected by it. Unlike section 87, schools were required to pay fees for registration, had to comply with detailed operating practices designed for children's homes and acquired a new legal status as homes which they felt to be alien to them. By contrast, the early experience of operating section 87 proved very positive. While the process was challenging and sometimes intrusive, both schools and SSDs believed that it enabled realistic scrutiny of welfare in schools. The feeling grew that something must be done to modify the impact of section 63. Some of the operating practices required (for example the keeping of a daily log of events) did not fit into school practice, while others (such as a personal visit to each child on entry to the school by the SSD) took insufficient account of the central role of the child's parents. Whatever their size, many began to argue that a school in which all the pupils returned home for the normal school holidays was simply a school and should be regulated by section 87. The status of being a children's home could be reserved for cases where care was provided on a more continuous basis.

Section 63

As it stands at present section 63 requires certain independent schools to register with the LASSD (Local Authority Social Services Department). It was inserted as a part of the gathering together of existing legislation, some of which had never been brought into force.

Section 63(6) reads:

> (6) An independent school is a children's home if-
>   (a) it provides accommodation for not more than fifty children; and
>   (b) it is not approved by the Secretary of State under section 11(3)(a) of the Education Act 1981.

Section 63 created a group of about 250 schools with more than three and less than 51 boarders. These schools must register annually with their LASSD as 'Children's Homes'. There is a marked diversity of school type in this category. Many are large day schools (600 or more on roll), with just a small boarding house for weekly boarders; others are small preparatory schools with numbers on roll of less than 70, most of whom are boarders. There are also small schools with 25 or less pupils, mostly boarders, catering wholly or mainly for pupils with special educational needs; these are schools which are not approved under the 1981 Act, several of which provide 52 week care.

An important distinction between most of the homes that are schools and those that are not is that parents have opted to send their children to the school and, in general, they pay school fees. This is in contrast to the general run of children's homes where children are usually *placed* by a LASSD. In these cases parents and children generally exercise no choice and the children usually come from background circumstances that necessitate placement away from home. Most of these children's homes do not provide education on site.

Volume 4 of the Guidance and Regulations concerned with *Residential Care* (dealing with sections 62, 63, 64 and 104) was published late in July 1991 for implementation, with the rest of the Act, on October 14th 1991.

At the time of writing, the Government was in consultation with schools and social services' interests about possible changes to the regulations which schools, required to register under section 63, must follow. If implemented, these would have the effect of removing from some schools, some of the requirements in the Children's Homes Regulations 1992, for example the need to keep a daily log or to preserve records for 75 years.

The schools affected would be those where the pupils normally return home to their parents in school holidays. In addition the same schools would be also excused the need to comply with the

Arrangements for Placements Regulations 1992, The Review of Children's Placements Regulations 1992 and the Representation Procedures Regulations 1992. Together, these would represent a significant reduction in the detailed burden of regulations for these schools but, of course, the duty to register under section 63 would remain in place, unless at some future point the Children Act itself were to be amended.

Section 87

Section 87 lays a duty on the proprietor of (or anyone else responsible for) any independent school which provides accommodation, to *safeguard and promote* the child's welfare (S87(1)). The Act (S87(3)) further lays a duty on the LASSD to: 'take such steps as are reasonably practicable to enable them to determine whether the child's welfare is adequately safeguarded and promoted while he is accommodated by the school', and empowers them to enter schools covered by section 87 at any reasonable time (S87(5)).

The Children Act brought with it amending legislation to create, for S87 schools, a fifth ground for complaint – that of welfare. Section 70 of the Education Act 1944 requires all independent schools to register with the Department For Education (DFE). Under section 71 of the 1944 Act a school may be found 'Objectionable' by the Secretary of State for Education on four grounds:

(a) that the school premises or any part of them are unsuitable for a school;

(b) that accommodation provided at the school premises is inadequate or unusable having regard to the number, ages and sex of the pupils attending the school;

(c) that efficient and suitable instruction is not being provided having regard to the number, ages and sex of the pupils attending the school;

(d) that the proprietor at the school or any of the teachers employed therein is not a proper person to be the proprietor or a teacher.

Schedule 13 of the Children Act amended the 1944 Education Act to create the fifth ground for complaint:

(e) there has been a failure, in relation to a child provided with accommodation by the school, to comply with the duty imposed by section 87 of the Children Act 1989 (welfare of children accommodated in independent schools).

If there is a failure under one or more of these headings the Secretary of State for Education can issue a Notice of Complaint (NOC) to the school. If this is not complied with the school could be removed from the register. The need to promote and safeguard welfare is a S87 duty and, although the Children Act is a Department of Health (DH) Act it falls to the DFE to deal with the NOC procedure.

The use of welfare as grounds for complaint only applies to S87 schools. In the case of S63 schools there are only the original four grounds for complaint. The LASSD, in dealing with an application for registration as a children's home, will be concerned only with those aspects of the school which are to do with being a children's home (that is, welfare matters). If it fails to satisfy the LASSD it will have its registration application refused and it will have to cease running its boarding element, appeal or face prosecution for carrying on an unregistered children's home.

Volume 5 of the Children Act statutory guidance, *Guidance and Regulations*, was published in mid May 1991 and affects about 550 mainstream independent schools with more than 50 boarders.[5] There are also about 70 special schools which *do* have fewer than 51 boarders, but which are approved under section 63 of the 1981 Education Act, and about 30 schools registered under the Registered Homes Act 1984 which come under the provisions of S87. There are only four S87 Regulations, far fewer than in the case of the S63 legislation. The first of these is the citation, commencement and interpretation. The second gives an authorised person the right to inspect any premises used by a relevant independent school, the third concerns inspection of individual children, and the last confers on the authorised person (inspecting officer) the right to inspect certain records if these are kept by the school.

The Practice Guide

Further guidance, *The Welfare of Children in Boarding Schools: Practice Guide,* was published in December 1991 and is complementary to the Volume 5 statutory guidance. It gives an outline of the relevant legislation, the roles of key agencies and the range of independent schools with boarding. It also discusses issues in developing LASSD practice, practice in boarding schools and the issue of LASSD reports on their contact with independent schools with boarding. This booklet was provided for LASSDs to assist in exercising their responsibilities for inspecting welfare in independent schools with boarding, and was written in such a way that it would prove of considerable use to governors, heads and staff in schools. It also provides guidance for LEAs, governors and schools with boarding in the maintained sector, including grant-maintained schools. Although the provisions of S63 and S87 do not apply to these schools, LEAs and governors may wish to make use of the guidance so that the welfare of boarding pupils in maintained schools is promoted and safeguarded.

Notes

1 *The Children Act 1989, The Welfare of Children in Boarding Schools, Practice Guide,* Department of Health Social Services Inspectorate, HMSO (1991).

2 *Independent Schools with Boarding — An induction framework for social services inspectors, trainers and managers,* Department of Health Social Services Inspectorate, HMSO (1992).

3 *School Life: Pupils' Views on Standards in Boarding School,* Dr Roger Morgan for the Department of Health Social Services' Inspectorate, HMSO; Provisional Title, to be published Autumn 1992.

4 *The Children Act 1989 Guidance and Regulations Volume 4 Residential Care,* Department of Health, HMSO (1991).

5 *The Children Act 1989 Guidance and Regulations Volume 5 Independent Schools,* Department of Health, HMSO (1991).

CHAPTER 2

The Children Act 1989 and Boarding: Practical Issues of Implementation

Brian P. FitzGerald HMI

The intention of the relevant sections of the Act is to secure the well-being of pupils who board. Many schools have, of course, developed features of excellence in the way they provide for their pupils, but the lessons of the parallel experience of looking after children in the social services field have generally not been available to them. There are also a number of good practice measures which have been found to be of special importance in reducing the likelihood that children will be abused and in developing effective responses to these unfortunate cases when prevention fails. A number of these are discussed in some detail in this chapter.

Welfare

Welfare is not defined in the Children Act, although in Volume 5 of the Guidance (paragraph 2.4.1) it is stated that:

> In safeguarding and promoting a child's welfare, proprietors need to be concerned with the health, happiness and proper physical, intellectual, emotional, social and behavioural development of that child as well, of course, as protecting him [her] against the risk of suffering significant harm or neglect.

It is difficult to separate welfare matters from those that are purely educational or which refer only to accommodation or premises. The context in which learning takes place can be a welfare matter. For example, behaviour and relationships in class, the conditions under which science experiments are carried out and the arrangements made for a geographical field course all have strong welfare implications.

Good practice in boarding

What is written about good welfare practice in the *Practice Guide* is closely related to many of the findings set out in *Boarding in Maintained Schools: A Survey*. In this document HMI state the complexities of what lies behind good provision:

> Good boarding provision necessarily consists of a complex and successful interplay of often very subtle factors. On the one hand there are the needs of the child in residence; these needs are as varied as the numbers concerned, and the provision of boarding is something of a compromise in attempting to meet the diversity of needs present at any one time. On the other hand what the school does in order to cater for these needs is equally complex in the opportunities it provides and constraints it places on the growth and development of the youngster.[1]

There is, therefore, always some tension between what is desirable for the welfare, growth and development of individual boarders, and what can be provided to meet their needs in what is essentially a communal setting. This is also reflected in a tension between the range of opportunities provided by the school for individual personal and social development, and the need to limit pupils' freedom of action in the interests of their safety, good behaviour and communal well-being.

Nevertheless, there are a number of important issues and needs for staff to consider and address. Some are immutable and mainly concern safety and protection; others, such as the 'fine line' between what constitutes 'proper' and 'improper' behaviour, are less clear and have no fixed markers. Not a great deal has been written about the issues central to good welfare practice in boarding, although this chapter attempts to define good practice in relation to the following:

- aims, objectives and guidelines for all who are concerned with the care welfare of boarders;
- training and induction of staff.

THE PROTECTIVE ELEMENT OF WELFARE:

- child protection procedures, including staff checks;
- appropriate confidentiality, and advocacy on behalf of boarders in trouble;

- a system for the resolution of grievances and complaints;
- access to 'independent listeners', to payphones in privacy, and the publication of telephone help lines;
- equal opportunities.

RELATIONSHIPS:

- staff relationships with boarders;
- levels of familiarity with boarders;
- a respect for privacy;
- relationships amongst boarders and the nature of peer groups;
- a school and house approach to all forms of bullying.

GROWING UP AND PREPARATION FOR THE NEXT STAGE:

- the personal, social, health and emotional growth of boarders;
- learning to take on responsibilities and make decisions;
- prefects and monitors: training for pastoral responsibility;
- boarders' preparation for the next stage of education and adulthood.

ACCOMMODATION:

- the nature of the boarders' environment.

The mission statement, aims and objectives, and guidelines

Consideration of each of these areas needs to be as much a part of the school's mission statement as its educational objectives, and the provision of a competent mission statement is a necessary part of effective management. There should be a clear statement of aims and objectives, both for the school as a whole, and for the residential experience it provides. It is also necessary to provide staff and boarders with guidelines about what is expected of them, and they should explain routines as well as giving details of rules, bounds, etc. Such documents will also provide others who need to know (for example, parents, governors and social services departments) with the basic information about boarding. These should include how the school provides for children's welfare, their physical and emotional growth, and their personal and social development. Chapter 3 explores these issues more fully.

Training and induction of staff

Maintaining and developing good welfare practice have implications for effective training, monitoring and appraisal of boarding staff and for appropriate induction of staff new to boarding. Paragraph 6.17 in the *Practice Guide* states:

> All staff, professional and others, involved in caring for children should have access to training to develop appropriate skills. All aspects of care should be covered in staff training including, in particular, counselling skills.

Training in listening to children and understanding their often hidden agendas, are important topics for in-service training. It is equally important that staff have training in how to speak to youngsters; so often poor relationships in a house stem from a member of staff not knowing how to do this.

The effective management of boarding necessarily requires monitoring of staff, not in a way that would inhibit the development of good, close and supportive relationships with boarders, but in a way that encourages an open and trusting society. Nevertheless senior staff need to be aware of the implications of stress arising from long hours on duty or heavy teaching commitments, the development of inappropriate relationships with individual boarders, and excessive volunteering for extra duties where the teacher is in an unsupervised one to one situation with boarders. It is also important that each member of the boarding staff has another colleague to whom he/she can turn to share experiences and talk through concerns and problems.

Boarding staff need to discuss, formally as well as informally, the effectiveness of boarding arrangements. Reviews and appraisal of the working of the house should be carried out on a termly or annual basis.

Staff new to boarding need, and have a right to expect, proper induction and support. Young staff in particular, not only new to boarding, but also coping with teaching for the first time, are particularly vulnerable to the emotional and physical pressures and stresses found in living in close proximity to young people.

The protective element of welfare

Child protection procedures

The school needs clearly documented procedures, based on those of the local Area Child Protection Committee (ACPC), which are in line with Volume 5 Guidance and advice given in section 5.20 of *Working Together*:

> All those involved with the provision of care for children in residential settings, including schools, must be alert to the possibility of abuse by other children, visitors and members of staff. Policies and managerial procedures must openly recognise the possibility of abuse and must prevent creating circumstances which could encourage abuse. There must be clear written procedures on how suspected abuse is to be dealt with, for children and staff to consult and available for external scrutiny.[2]

These procedures need to appear in the school's guidelines, with additional references in any house-specific sets of documents. It is very important that staff fully understand the procedures.

It is also important that child protection issues are represented in the school's curriculum from the first year a boarder is in the school. *Working Together* states that:

> Schools ... have a role in preventing abuse through the curriculum. They can help pupils and students to acquire relevant information, skills and attitudes both to resist abuse in their own lives and to prepare them for the responsibilities of their adult lives, including parenthood. Some schools include specific teaching about the risks of child abuse and how pupils can protect themselves, within their personal and social education programmes.[3]

Boarders should be aware of some aspects of the child protection procedures, for instance, the opportunity to talk to adults in private about concerns they may have. Such information could be provided along with any leaflets produced for boarders on the school's complaints procedure.

Where there is good practice, boarding staff are prepared to reinforce the messages in their informal talks with boarders.

Other aspects of child protection include the very necessary procedures to do with the checking of newly appointed staff, or those already employed taking on new roles. These refer to those *who have significant contact with boarders.* Such procedures include applying to the DFE, or other authorised holders of the list, for checks against List 99, with the DH Consultancy Service and, in the case of teachers and others with significant contact with pupils, with the DFE, for any criminal record. Not only should teaching staff and those with direct care responsibilities be checked, but also those who have significant contact with children, especially if this is on a one-to-one basis. This may, on occasion include gardeners, etc. The DFE letter to the heads and proprietors of all independent schools, dated 30 April 1990 gives further details.

It is essential that heads and staff are clear about the procedures, and that they are trained to recognise the signs of abuse. It is also important that headteachers and house staff identify human and physical situations that could lead to abuse and that, wherever possible, such risky situations are taken into account in organisation and management procedures.

Listening and talking

A willingness to listen to children is essential and staff must make time to be with boarders to do this. There is prime time here as in any family. This includes time sitting with children at meals, walking with them across a playground or around the grounds, and time sitting and chatting with them on the edge of a bed in a bedroom or dormitory. Although this is often most usefully arrived at casually, staff must recognise its crucial importance. Formal time spent on duty (for example, patrolling dormitories in an evening) is not always the best time for informal contact, as the member of staff will need to have his or her attention on many things. Schools generally realise that all staff (matrons, domestic staff, ground staff as well as teachers and care staff) may be approached by boarders to talk to and act as confidants.

Staff must not only be prepared to make time to be with boarders, but they must also learn to listen to them and communicate with them. A common cause of problems in a house is the inability of house staff to communicate effectively with the boarders.

Confidentiality

When staff are approached by a child in distress or with a problem they must understand that a child's opening remarks may cover something of greater importance and concern to him or her. While confidentiality is of the utmost importance, particularly for the child, all boarders must realise that not everything they may raise can be kept confidential. The art of negotiating the outcome of what a child may have yet to say, is an art learnt with difficulty by staff. It is not possible to keep confidence at the expense of a child. In a situation such as this, the very fact a boarder has come to a teacher to talk through a serious concern usually indicates that he or she is more than willing for some action to be taken.

Advocacy

Where there are good relationships, the house tutor with care and pastoral responsibilities for a boarder will be prepared to act as advocate whenever there are, for example, discipline problems outside the confines of the tutorial or house. A child with problems with 'authority' or with other members of staff, needs an adult prepared to support him or her, even if it is shown that the child is guilty of some serious misdemeanour. The advocate role is a difficult one for many care staff to take on as it may appear as undue support for a miscreant or trouble-maker against other members of staff.

Resolution of grievances and complaints

Inevitably there will be grumbles and complaints from boarders; in most instances these can be resolved by talking them through. The Volume 5 Guidance requires that there is an effective means by which children's complaints can be heard (paragraph 3.11.1). There should be a rather more formal procedure for raising problems or making a complaint; procedures which are easily understood by boarders. In a school where relationships are good and there is an open and trusting atmosphere such procedures will rarely be invoked. Indeed it could be argued that learning to understand (and use sensibly) such a procedure is both a basic right and an important element in the functioning of a secure and confident community.

Access to independent listeners and helplines

Independent listeners

Access to adults independent of the school, to whom boarders can turn if they feel they need a completely impartial ear, is essential

(Volume 5 Guidance, paragraph 3.11.1). Such 'independent listeners' need to be vetted in the same way as other staff who have significant contact with children. They should not be teachers, but it is useful for them to be seen about the school from time to time attending school functions. They, accompanied by their partners, could also be invited to house functions.

Telephones and helplines

There should be facilities to ensure that children can maintain contact with parents, relatives and friends in privacy, for example by the use of suitably placed payphones (see Volume 5 Guidance, paragraph 3.7). There may be problems with young boarders phoning home, particularly in the first few weeks after joining the school. This may cause acute home-sickness, but such problems are normally resolved very quickly in a warm and caring house.

Advertising helplines such as Childline is strongly recommended in the *Practice Guide* (paragraph 6.25). Access to Childline by boarders does not undermine respect or authority. There is little evidence to suggest that boarders use helplines frivolously or to harm their teachers or other staff. They do provide the very important service of an independent and confidential listener with whom children who are worried or in distress about *any* matter can discuss their concerns.

The range of problems raised by callers to Childline's *Boarding School Line* was very wide, with bullying topping the list.[4] This accounted for about 20 per cent of the 1,000 or so calls that resulted in some form of counselling. Sexual abuse accounted for about 15 per cent, but calls about problems to do with friendships, parents, staff, homesickness, problems with work, punishment, personal sexuality, drugs and medical matters, together accounted for about a third of calls.

Equal opportunities

Boarders may well spend 60 per cent or more of their adolescent lives in the care of adults who are not their parents. It is therefore incumbent upon care staff to prepare them for living in a society that is multi-ethnic, multicultural, contains both women and men with equal rights, has a proportion of its population that is disabled in some way, has people from a wide background of class and many whose sexual orientation is not the same as theirs. In all these cases the school needs, in its curriculum, and more informally in the house, to be aware of the importance attached to teaching youngsters to avoid: group-stereotyping, isolating individuals for whatever reason, making racist or sexist jokes or jokes about disabled people, and striking macho attitudes. All these, and other areas, need to be fully talked through with the boarders by house staff, who need to react immediately to any offensive racist or other remark made in the house or elsewhere.

A particular issue in most houses is that of the display of inappropriate posters in bedrooms and study areas. It is not enough to use just the yardstick of 'whether you would be happy for the cleaner to see it' (possibly itself a sexist comment), but of much greater importance is the way in which staff use this to tackle the issue of attitudes to girls (or boys) and of what constitutes 'bad taste'.

Relationships

Staff relationships with boarders

The existence of good relationships is the key to good boarding. A boarding house needs to have an open and trusting ethos; among boarders, between staff and boarders and among staff. If this is present then difficulties can all the more easily be resolved, bullying and harassment are not likely to be a major concern and the conditions that could lead to abuse in one form or another are less likely to be present.

The *Practice Guide* states (paragraph 6.44) that:

> Staff relationships with boarders ... must be warm and supportive, and capable of celebrating achievement, providing support, anticipating problems and dealing with disciplinary matters sensibly and fairly. [Staff] must be prepared to provide support and comfort during times when there may be stress at school, worry about problems at home or home-sickness.

It is important that boarding staff listen to boarders and talk with them. Staff have to be sensitive to what children are really saying, and must be prepared to provide support and advice over a wide range of problems and concerns. These may include problems with friendships and to do with work, concerns about home circumstances, their own physical development and sexuality, and perhaps relationships with individual members of staff.

Familiarity between staff and boarders

All staff, particularly teachers and others new to residential care, should be aware of the fine boundary between what is appropriate support, care and friendship for children on the one hand, and an excessive degree of intimacy on the other. The line between what is 'proper' and what is not in any particular situation is blurred, and closely related to the general ethos of the school; its position could well be very different in two schools of contrasting character. In any one school, however, the line should be consistent and not the cause of unpleasant comparison between houses.

There is a second boundary in this model, the line between what is and what is not criminal behaviour. This line does not vary, although, in judgement, it is a matter for legal process.

Boarding staff may be worried that close and supportive relationships with boarders might be misconstrued, especially in light of publicity given to child protection matters, but it would be quite wrong for such concerns to prevent appropriately warm and supportive relationships developing between boarders and staff.

Some staff fear that such matters as hugging and one to one contact is no longer possible. It is important that staff feel they can comfort boarders under stress and talk to children in private, but they need to recognise there may be times when they may be vulnerable (for example, where children are emotionally or behaviourally disturbed, or where it is necessary for a member of staff to interview an individual child), or where there is regular close one to one contact (as in the case of individual music lessons).

Clearly there need to be stated and understood procedures concerning physical contact and interviews. These could include, for example, realising the sense in hugging a child sideways on, keeping ajar the door of the room where a meeting is taking place, and only doing so when other members of staff are around and could knock and enter.

In a similar vein, there need to be accepted procedures about the times male (or female) staff have access to girls (or boys) boarding areas; a particularly important matter for the spouses of house staff. This is a difficult area because there are numerous factors to be taken into account: the age and maturity of the boarders; the time of the evening; whether chaperoning is possible; whether the adult is resident (and well known to the boarders) or non-resident (and less well known); or whether the visitor is a stranger to the house.

A respect for privacy

In all cases it is important that boarders' feelings and privacy are respected. This is particularly important concerning entry to bedrooms. There should be no 'no-go' areas in the house or school at large, but basic conventions concerning entering a person's private space (for example, by knocking on doors) should always be observed. In return staff should also expect to receive the privacy that they and their families are due.

Peer groups and relationships among boarders

Good relationships among boarders are an essential element of good quality welfare. A happy and friendly house promotes boarders' personal and emotional development and is instrumental in enabling appropriate academic development. Boarders who live under stressful conditions because of difficulties with their peers or with adults with whom they come into daily contact are not only going to be miserable but are likely to underachieve academically and may be emotionally affected for much of their lives.

It is important that boarding staff are sensitive to friendship patterns in the house and school. This is particularly so in respect to spotting changes that occur in these patterns and noticing boarders who are or become isolated by their peers. Isolation is debilitating and can cause a considerable degree of misery, it often precedes more obvious bullying.

There is a close correlation between the quality of peer-group relationships and the quality of the relationships between staff and boarders. If there are problems between the house staff and boarders there is a tendency for boarder peer groups to become very strong, often as a form of defence. This can have the result that some boarders, who are perhaps in some way different from the others, are excluded from friendship and the all-important information-sharing groups. Such pupils may become prone to bullying and as a result enter a cycle of social and academic deprivation with long-lasting and profoundly deleterious effects. Further discussion of this area is taken up in Chapter 7.

Good relationships are also indicated by the extent to which younger boarders turn to older for advice and comfort at times of stress and home-sickness. It is quite right for older boarders to be prepared to take on this responsibility, and house staff should actively encourage this as growth in taking responsibility for others. Staff need to take the opportunity to discuss with older boarders what are appropriate levels of contact between older and younger pupils.

A house and school approach to all forms of bullying

Bullying is probably as endemic in boarding as it is in schools and society at large. Staff need to be very clear about what constitutes bullying, including as it does: persistent teasing or name calling, racial or sexual harassment, emotional abuse, extortion, or outright physical abuse. The school needs to address the issue in its curriculum through, for example, any personal, social and health education (PSHE) course run by the school, and the issue needs to be clearly taken on board in its policy documents and guidance. There is need for a continuing approach to bullying, with the issue being raised within peer groups, tackled in discussion and by role-play so that the group accept what is going on and begin to feel what it is like to be bullied. It is important that moves towards its eradication become a social group responsibility.

In the *Practice Guide* (paragraph 6.51) it is suggested that bullying tends to thrive where:

> there is inadequate presence of staff around the house, in the bedrooms and around the grounds;
> there is boredom, often bred of lack of purpose within the house or school;
> there is crowding in dormitories and bedrooms, or lack of common room space or lack of space for boarders to withdraw from the hurly burly of boarding life;
> there is not an open and trusting society;
> boarders feel unable to share their problems with staff;
> in respect to a prefectorial body or senior boarders:
>> there is a near complete delegation of house duties and control to them;
>> there is little supervision of their duties;
>> there has been little or no training or preparation for such responsibilities;

there has been little realisation on the part of the staff of the broader pastoral context of the role of prefects.

Where there is good boarding practice the ethos of a house is such that boarders are happy to bring instances of bullying to light; and they should be strongly encouraged to do so. Young lives can be tortured, suicide contemplated and even carried through in the more extreme cases as a result of bullying. At the very least bullying inflicts extreme unhappiness on a child, scars him or her emotionally, and causes marked under-performance in academic work. Staff will realise that in boarding there is no escape after school for a victim.

In some schools and houses, staff may feel there is no incidence of bullying; this may be so, but if the house or school embarked upon a confidential survey of boarders, they may find that all is not as it appears to be. In this matter house staff, and the school generally, must not be complacent.

Bullying was the single most important problem raised by callers to Childline's Boarding School Line, accounting for one-fifth of all the calls.[5] Bullying was also the subject of a dedicated Bullying Line, and the Gulbenkian Foundation, last year, published the results of Professor Jean La Fontaine's analysis of telephone calls to Childline about bullying.[6] This research also included calls made by children to Boarding School Line. Boarding house staff need to be aware of the nature of the problems raised by children in their calls to Childline, which are discussed in both these booklets.

In dealing with bullying, staff will act quickly, but with sensitivity. The victim(s) will require support, the class group or tutorial will need counselling and the perpetrator(s) will also require counselling and support, perhaps with the aid of an outside agency. Where either or both the victim(s) and the perpetrator(s) move to other schools as a result of the incidents, the receiving school needs to be fully aware of the circumstances and be prepared to provide appropriate support and counselling where this is needed.

Growing up and preparation for the next stage

Personal, health, social and emotional development of boarders

Staff need to be fully aware of the implications of having children from 7 to 11 or 13, and from 11 or 13 to 18 in their care for 60 or

70 per cent of their adolescent lives. Each arrives in the system as a pre-adolescent child and leaves — if he or she stays the course — as a fully developed male or female adult with most of the rights and responsibilities of adulthood.

It is essential that the school recognises its responsibilities and provides, over this period of growth, for the range of needs for each child's development. This will enable each boarder to learn to cope successfully with a range of challenges and increasing responsibilities, appropriate to his or her age and maturity. In the sixth-form, for example, it is likely that boarders will have a great deal of responsibility for running their own affairs, both individually and as a body, and for looking after younger boarders.

Learning to take on responsibilities and make decisions

Taking responsibilities
Good practice will involve the school and house in planning for the boarder's growth and development through the care they provide and in the way they encourage taking responsibilities for their own affairs, their health and their environment. Progressively they will provide opportunities for taking responsibility for others. Planning for providing for growth in responsibility should be clearly set out in the school's aims and boarding guidelines.

Learning to take responsibilities in these areas is a right. Success is seen in the way pupils work in the classroom, how older boarders look after younger, how they treat the school environment and how they relate to each other and to visitors.

Learning to make decisions
Of great importance is the need for boarders to be consulted and involved in decision-making about their own circumstances and to be encouraged to contribute to discussion about their general care and welfare. Growth in ability to make reasoned decisions and to challenge, when necessary, is of fundamental importance in personal development; this should be clearly stated in boarding guidelines and seen to be effective in the life of the house.

The school needs to provide particular forums where pupils can have a chance to share in corporate decision-making and feel that they are being consulted adequately. Schools vary in their approach to this, several have 'councils' for particular age groups or houses, others have a range of committees on which there are pupil-representatives or which are run by the pupils themselves (for example, dining-room committee, rules committee, etc). For older pupils, especially sixth-formers, there is usually a range of social and other committees for which the students are responsible themselves. In all these instances it is important that *staff and senior management* are seen to consider these to be important and to offer advice and encouragement as necessary. Most should have a formal basis (with agendas, minutes, etc) and action should be seen to result, even if it is only a detailed explanation why something cannot be done.

Such pupil involvement in consultation, discussion and decision-making should be seen as important even with the youngest who, for example, may be part of a group who inspect the boarding house once each half-term with the head of house and the clerk of works to audit the state of the fabric. To participate in committees and discussion groups such as this should be seen as an important element in a boarder's education and personal development.

Prefects and monitors: training for pastoral responsibility

In the same way it is very reasonable for older boarders to take on some degree of formal responsibility for younger through a monitor or prefect system. Where responsibilities are given to older boarders they must be prepared for their responsibilities and have some degree of training for their duties. But it should not be just a matter of duties, they should also be prepared to take on the pastoral aspects of being an older girl or boy with responsibilities in the house. Here too, there needs to be full and frank discussion with the older boarders about their attitudes towards, and contacts with, younger pupils in taking on these responsibilities. Even where older boarders do not have formal responsibilities of this sort, it is still essential that they have the opportunity to discuss with staff their approach to, and relationship with, younger boarders.

Some schools have instigated leadership training for all their lower sixth, involving the pastoral aspects of leadership. Clearly some older boarders will not wish to exercise such leadership; this should be accepted only with reluctance as it is every young person's right and need to take an increasing responsibility, and schools should plan this into their pastoral curriculum. In such cases, however, it may be possible to provide responsibilities of a different kind. In all circumstances it is important that staff effectively monitor what older boarders do, and under no circumstances should prefects have unlimited and completely unsupervised access to younger, and perhaps more vulnerable, boarders.

The staff must also be conscious of the pressures that such older boarders can be subjected to, especially at times approaching public examinations. Tutors must be particularly sensitive to this issue and must monitor the often conflicting demands being made on the individuals in their group.

Preparation for the next stage

The responsibilities that the school and the house have for shaping the future character and emotional well-being are very great. It is therefore very important that in its statement of aims and objectives the school includes references to the ways in which it intends to provide opportunities for the boarders to develop responsibilities for self, for others and for their environment; how they will be prepared for coping with life in a senior school, or college, or in a job; how the school intends to provide for sex education, for learning to follow a healthy lifestyle, for understanding drugs misuse, the dangers of smoking and alcohol abuse.

It is very likely that the school will be addressing many or all of these intentions in its timetabled curriculum, but the informal role of house and care staff, and the medical staff is crucial. There must be close co-operation and understanding between whoever manages the curriculum input and those who are responsible for the care and welfare of the boarders in order to make such intentions effective.

Accommodation

The nature of the boarders' environment[7]

Matters to do with accommodation are central to many welfare issues in boarding and, of course, the health and safety of boarders while accommodated by a school are of paramount importance. In Volume 5 of the Guidance (paragraph 3.4.1) it is stated:

> The nature and use of accommodation in all premises occupied by pupils should be such as to allow them to live a full life in

> the school community. .... [Accommodation] should be pleasant, comfortable, safe and geared to the child's needs.

The needs of children for privacy, to have access to quiet places to which they can retreat when they wish to be alone or in small groups and to take part in various forms of recreation, are all matters of priority in providing for children's development, both socially and emotionally. They need to be able to personalise their private space, such as around their bed or in their study area, and have a place to store their personal items safely, free from interference from others.

Volume 5 of the Guidance (paragraph 3.4.2) states that personal space is important to young people's social well-being, and that:

> boarders need to be able to:
>
> a) personalise those areas which they can regard as their own ...;
> b) store their personal possessions in their own lockable cupboard or chest of drawers;
> c) enjoy a degree of privacy, when they can be alone, withdraw in pairs or small groups from the hurly-burly of communal life, to read, talk, be quiet, do nothing, withdraw from younger/older peers;
> d) withdraw, in mixed schools, from those of the opposite sex; and
> e) have access to appropriate staff in private.

The overall quality of the boarders' environment is also an important element in the young person's growing awareness of and sensitivity to environmental quality. So often this can be dulled or rendered insensitive by poor cleaning, scruffy decoration, dilapidated furniture, and generally poor examples set by adults in running the house. This can easily lead to rejection of social responsibility and even vandalism. Good practice in a house is found where staff:

> a) set a good example in terms of tidiness and reasonable order;
> b) insist on effective cleaning and on the provision of reasonable quality furnishing;
> c) discuss with all age groups matters to do with the maintenance of the quality of their own space and that of the house as a whole; and

d) encourage an active participation by boarders in decision-making and thinking about changes affecting their house.

Finally, being a carer or a boarding house person requires enormous reserves of energy, tact, sensitivity and a wide range of skills. A carer also needs to have enthusiasm, a strong sense of humour, and above all a very real empathy for the young people they have in their care. These characteristics are not easily acquired, although many boarding staff appear to have been born with super-human reserves of just these qualities. Hours of duty may be prescribed, but the resident matron, housemaster or housemistress is always on duty and liable to be called out even in the early hours to attend to a sick child. Even on the evening off duty, how often would we hear: 'Hello Sir, I know it is late and that it is your evening off, so I thought it would be a good time to catch you to discuss my UCCA form'? Perhaps we could substitute any of the following for 'discuss my UCCA form'

'say that James has just been sick all over the corridor ...'
'tell you that Glynn's rats have escaped from their cage in the dormitory'
'let you know Mary has not returned from her trip to Dorking'
'ask you why the hot water boiler isn't working again'
'warn you that there seems to be a prowler in the grounds ...'
'introduce you to Mr Jones of the Social Services' Department'.

Notes

1 *Boarding in Maintained Schools: A survey (a report by HMI),* DES (1990), (Reference 211/90/NS), Appendix A, opening paragraph.
2 *Working Together under the Children Act 1989: A guide to arrangements for inter-agency co-operation for the protection of children from abuse,* HMSO (1991). Section 5.20, Children in Residential Settings refers.
3 *Working Together under the Children Act 1989,* Section 4.39.
4 *Boarding School Line, a summary of the results of an experimental helpline for boarding school pupils, January – July 1991,* pp. 6 – 7 and table opposite p. 6, DES (1992).
5 *Boarding School Line, a summary,* op cit above.
6 *Bullying: the child's view, an analysis of telephone calls to Childline about bullying,* Jean La Fontaine, Calouste Gulbenkian Foundation, 1991.
7 General guidance on the minimum standards of accommodation in boarding is currently contained in Part IV of the *Education (Standards for School Premises) Regulations 1981,* HMSO, (SI 1981, No. 909), but at time of going to press is subject to review.

CHAPTER 3

The Aims of Residential Education and Care

Ewan Anderson

Introduction

The basic necessity identified in *The Children Act 1989, Guidance and Regulations, Volume 5 Independent Schools* (paragraph 3.1.1) is that: 'The school must have a clear statement of principles on which the life of the school is based.' For a boarding school, this immediately raises the question, *What is boarding education*? Traditionally and perhaps ideally, boarding education is seen as the totality of the provision, both in the classroom and outside it. This is commonly underlined by the dual role of the house or boarding staff who are also teachers. Boarding education is thus seen as the complete process, everything that occurs within the boarding school.

The fundamental aims of all schools, whether boarding or day, are the same, but boarding schools have in many ways a greater opportunity to achieve them. The Education Reform Act (1988) states that:

> The curriculum should be 'balanced and broadly based' and should
>
> (a) promote the spiritual, moral, cultural, mental and physical development of pupils at the school and of society; and
> (b) prepare pupils for the opportunities, responsibilities and experiences of adult life.

These aims are expressed more fully in the schools' curriculum statement which, in addition to a consideration of aims and values, provides guidance on content and organisation, learning experience and achievements, outcome and evaluation (Council of Local Education Authorities (CLEA), 1990). The contents section should include planning across subjects, cross-curricular skills (for example, communication, problem-solving skills, personal and social skills), personal and social education and cross-curricular themes (for example, health education, careers education, citizenship). Linked to personal and social education, but distinct from it, is the policy on pastoral care and guidance. Such a policy must include a code of behaviour and provision for:

(a) links with parents and guardians and the local community;
(b) guidance and counselling on learning, personal problems and relationships; and
(c) an atmosphere conducive to learning.

The subjects can be located in the nine generally accepted areas of experience: physical, human and social, moral and spiritual, aesthetic and creative, linguistic and literary, mathematical, scientific, and technological. Thus, from the level of the curriculum statement down to that of the individual subject, a common theme of personal and social development can be traced.

For day pupils, a major part of their personal and social development occurs outside school hours and is the responsibility of their parents or guardians. For boarders, for a large part of the year, the school assumes that responsibility. Therefore, although personal and social education may not be seen as totally congruent with boarding education, it must provide a very significant component to it.

However, the distinction between boarding and day is becoming increasingly blurred. Most boarding schools have at least some day pupils and for many, the day proportion is high and increasing. In some cases, an extended day is adopted, with day pupils arriving immediately after breakfast and departing late in the evening. As a result, day pupils are able to share the boarding ethos without actually sleeping in the school. This raises the interesting issue as to whether such a day pupil receives a boarding education.

At the same time, but for different reasons, many day schools of various kinds are also using an extended day. For reasons frequently connected with travel, extra tuition or extra-curricular activities, some pupils will arrive well before the start of morning school and leave in the evening. Even if they receive breakfast and perhaps some sort of evening meal, their education, although obviously more complete than that of the normal day pupil, would not be categorised as boarding education. Therefore, although the difference between them is declining and their overall aims are the same, there remains a major distinction between day and boarding schools. At one level, this is merely that boarders sleep and have their breakfast in the school. At a more important level is the question of commitment. For a boarder, the boarding house is their 'home from home', for a large part of the year, it is their home base. Whether it is a separate room or merely a bed space, territorial instincts usually become apparent. There is a tendency to personalise the space and, once personalised, to defend it. Personalised and defended, it becomes the refuge for the individual, where he can enjoy the territorial satisfactions of security, identity and stimulation (Porteous, 1977). Thus, psychologically, day school and boarding education are very different. The dependence of the boarder upon the school is far greater and relationships with at least some members of staff are likely to be closer. These two factors can be illustrated by quotations from very different sources.

In *Good Enough Parenting* (Central Council for Education and Training in Social Work, 1978) dependence is in evidence when the significance of everyday events is considered:

> Imagine a single meal time; a child will have learnt something from it; it will have been a more or less nourishing experience, physically and emotionally, according to whether he enjoyed the food and company, or whether the experience was stressful because adults were largely concerned with table manners and may have punished him if he dared to criticise their good food or failed to leave a clean plate. One meal time is perhaps neither here nor there; however, three meals a day over a period of weeks, months or years, plus a dozen other routine aspects are surely very cumulative in their effect.

An Experience of Teaching (Lucas, 1975) focuses upon experience in a small boarding grammar school in which the author was able to examine, in practical terms, what is meant by boarding education and, particularly, the relationships involved:

> In talking to my pupils, especially the older ones, about personal relationships we discussed, among other questions, why argument

so often seems to intensify rather than to settle differences, and why at a certain point in conversation one really knows that there is no possibility of coming nearer agreement. This happens when what one might think of as the essence, whether of community or of individual personality is threatened. I tried to imagine this necessary web of assurance and security on which the pupils who came to see me depended.

Thus, it is clear that while all schools must share the same overall goals, especially with regard to personal and social education, education in boarding schools, possibly distinguished as 'boarding education' bears a greater responsibility for personal and social development. This is recognised in *The Welfare of the Children in Boarding Schools: Practice Guide* (Social Services Inspectorate, 1991), which stresses that the statement of principles on which the life of the school is based should:

> Include a clear set of aims for the provision of boarding. There should also be clear guidelines and procedures for boarding that are not just statements of details of organisation. They should be complementary to the school's aims and objectives and to its pastoral guidelines, and should allow the successful achievement of aims and objectives to be assessed.

Furthermore, detailed suggestions are listed of topics which should be included in the guidelines:

(a) matters affecting the welfare and education of boarders and including a section on the induction of new boarders;

(b) the contribution boarding life makes to boarders' personal and social development while they are in the school;

(c) the way boarding contributes to fitting boarders for independence and self-reliance as young adults;

(d) equal opportunities in ethnic, cultural, linguistic, religious, gender and disability matters;

(e) the contribution that boarding staff make to the health education of boarders and promotion of a healthy lifestyle with particular respect to alcohol and drug abuse, smoking, physical and emotional development, and healthy eating;

(f) action to be taken should abuse be suspected or allegations of abuse be made;

(g) complaints procedures appropriate to the age groups concerned;

(h) the school's disciplinary measures, including guidance on actions to be taken should bullying or other forms of harassment be alleged; and

(i) daily and weekend routines, signing-out procedures and other organisational matters, the location of 'bounds', and where pupils of different ages may go unaccompanied, in pairs or in groups during their leisure time.

Aims and objectives

A statement of aims and objectives has become such an accepted part of the educational scene that the rationale behind their formulation is often overlooked. The construction of worthwhile aims and objectives for boarding education possess obvious difficulties since many of the desired outcomes must be, by their nature, subjective. Therefore, to ease the situation and clarify the construction procedure, it is useful to rehearse some of the earlier arguments which laid the ground rules.

Before any aims or objectives can be considered, there needs to be some preliminary analysis (Figure 1). Clearly, the range and scope of the content must be examined, particularly in such an all embracing field as personal and social development. For skills, a behavioural definition is comparatively straightforward, but for concepts or principles, at least part of the definition may need to be subjective. Furthermore, in the case of boarding education, training may be seen as only a first stage, achievement occurring through experience in the real world. In examining content in a broad, general framework, Rowntree (1974) lists three sources:

(a) expectations about the future needs of society;

(b) analysis of the opinions, practices and writing of experts; and

(c) analysis of the structure of the subject matter itself and its relevance to the interests of the pupil.

The need for the curriculum to fit pupils for a place in society has already been noted. While there are experts in boarding education itself, it is possible to draw on expertise from across the complete spectrum of residential education and care in other services and settings. With regard to the interests of the pupils, a key focus must be the needs of children.

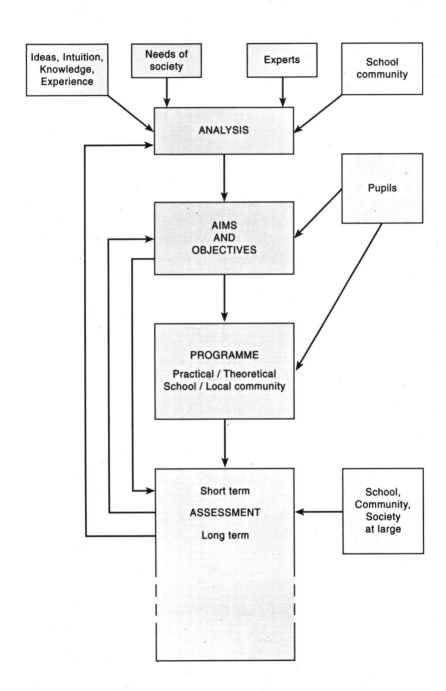

Figure 1   Aims and objectives in context

Once selected, the content must be examined in the light of any particular group of boarders with regard to age, aptitude, ability and motivation. Potential learning and teaching difficulties need to be identified, but, perhaps more importantly, the starting point or level of pre-knowledge. The baseline indicates not only the starting point for the education envisaged, but it also provides a measure against which development can be assessed. Furthermore, there is strong evidence that as a result of personal and social education, pupils pass through a number of well-defined developmental stages (Hunt and Sullivan, 1974) and it is vital to know the stage which each pupil has reached.

A further aspect in the analysis is the learning environment, a term susceptible to widely varying interpretation. However, since boarding education is thought to result from the complete experience of living in the school, the totality of that environment is clearly crucial. From personalised bed spaces to the behaviour of the peer group, the role of staff as models and the traditions of the school, all are significant. Residential education is a product of 'shared-life-space' (Redl, 1966).

Lastly, even during the preliminary analysis, some thought should be given as to the possible standards which might be achieved. Given the boarder group and the learning environment, these need to be realistic and related to requirements in the outside world. Apart from the obvious query as to what are the standards of the outside world, this raises the interesting question of whether or not social and personal development achieved in boarding education should attempt to set the prevailing standards. This would presumably follow if training for leadership is considered part of boarding education.

With the analysis completed, attention can be given to the desired learning outcomes, which can be seen, at a minimal level, as serving three main functions:

(a) indicating direction for teaching and more long-term curriculum development;
(b) providing a framework for assessment; and
(c) acting as a further aid to learning.

In the short term, stated outcomes are directional in that they allow a realistic estimate to be made of the course content, which can be structured according to the relevance and significance of particular topics. Since lower level outcomes can be synthesised to produce those of a more general nature, a sequencing of material is also suggested. They can also be used as indicators of the appropriate teaching methods. In the longer term, as a statement of intention, outcomes facilitate co-operative thinking and planning among teachers.

However, the major benefit of formulating outcomes is that they indicate methods of assessment and assessment can provide not only a guide to pupil progress, but also an evaluation of programme effectiveness. Finally, it would seem self-evident that pupils will learn more efficiently if they have a picture of the overall programme. This also introduces the important issue of pupil contribution to the framing of outcomes. Since boarding education is essentially community based and iterative, pupils are particularly well placed to assist in improving the statement of outcomes.

Having examined the potential benefits which may accrue from a carefully worded statement of intention, the terminology needs to be considered. Aims and objectives, together with other similar terms, are frequently used interchangeably, despite the fact that there are obvious advantages in distinguishing between them and general agreement has been reached on definitions. For example, Gronlund (1970), Rowntree (1974) and Stewart (1975) all, implicitly or explicitly designate as aims, high level statements which provide an overall guide, but cannot by their nature be directly evaluated, and as objectives, statements at a generally lower level, but possessing their own inbuilt assessment. Aims indicate a general direction for learning and it should be possible to monitor progress, but the final outcome, for reasons such as its subjective nature, defies precise assessment. A statement such as 'to develop independence' is an aim. While certain changes in behaviour may indicate that personal and social development is moving in the appropriate direction, independence is a relative term and it cannot be indicated by behaviour alone. Complete independence, for obvious reasons, cannot be achieved in a boarding school nor even in society. Thus, the aim acts as a signpost, pointing over the horizon, indicating a course, but not a precise destination.

In contrast, objectives are attainable, are specific and are normally couched in behavioural terms. As a result, their achievement can be objectively assessed. Objectives such as 'to appear neatly and correctly dressed' or 'to display acceptable table manners' can be written in behavioural terms, with tightly defined standards. However, this is a somewhat pedantic process and is probably unnecessary in that, while there is an element of subjectivity, there would be general agreement on what are acceptable table manners. The important point is that the improvement of table manners involves a definite behaviour change which can be measured. Less obviously, objectives about relationships with peers or showing responsibility for work, although they focus upon a mental change, none the less involve observable behaviour. Thus, objectives, even if not tightly specified, place an emphasis on what is overt and allow monitoring procedures to be developed. They also provide, as is clear from the examples given, milestones along the route to the achievement of the aims.

However, given the wide-ranging aims of boarding education, it would seem that only relatively trivial learning could be described by highly specific, easily tested objectives. Furthermore, since a significant part of the assessment is likely to be subjective, it is clear that a balance must be struck somewhere between the classical behavioural objectives and loosely structured aims. As a result, assessment will be less clear-cut, but it will be possible to monitor the main milestones indicating progress towards the aim. The important point is that in constructing such hybrid objectives, the possibilities for assessment are borne in mind.

Using the classification of Eraut (1973), the desired outcomes should be, as far as possible, observable, planned, desirable and important. At the same time, it is realised that there will be unobservable results and advantage should be taken of desirable or important unplanned outcomes.

There is also a time factor to be considered, since both aims can be long term or short term. In general, objectives would tend to be short term and aims longer term. In boarding education, many of the aims must be long term in that they refer to life after school in society. In fact, it would be claimed by some that what is instilled in boarding education lasts for life. As one headmaster of a well-known Catholic boarding school observed when asked about the aims of the education provided: 'we prepare our boys for death'.

In the best-known taxonomy, objectives are divided into three domains; the cognitive (Bloom, 1956), the affective (Krathwohl *et al.*, 1964) and the psychomotor. This has now been modified into the more familiar areas of knowledge, attitudes and skills. At the lower levels within each category, it is relatively easy to construct behavioural or at least tightly structured objectives, but at the higher levels, outcomes may be more effectively formulated as aims. For example, in the category of knowledge, comprehension is relatively easy to assess, whereas evaluation is far more complex and subjective. Indeed, it has been shown (Anderson, 1975) that there is a need for a higher level category which is an amalgam of elements from the other three. This category, 'modes of personal operation' includes ideas such as receptiveness, creativeness, awareness and reflection. For example, in boarding education, the development of group sensitivity is one such desired outcome. An awareness of feelings and possible responses within a community involves the subtle interplay of personalities and the 'whole' person at a deep level.

In conclusion, a useful distinction can be made between aims and objectives, but as Hogben (1972) observed, 'We should state course objectives by all means, but we should not insist that they are all framed in highly specific behavioural terms.' The most effective approach would seem to be to produce a statement of aims and then to subdivide these into objectives, bearing in mind the importance of assessment. It is important that the aggregation of objectives facilitates monitoring along the route to the achievement of the aim.

The needs of children

In formulating aims for boarding education, a basic starting point would be the needs of children. The subject has obviously been widely considered, but probably the most useful and complete discussion occurs in Kellmer-Pringle (1980), while the most succinct statement is the United Nations Declaration of the Rights of the Child. The National Council of Voluntary Child Care Organizations (NCVCCO) presents in *A Statement on Principles and Practices in Work with Children, Young People and Families* (undated), a summary of the fundamental needs of children, expressed as rights:

(a) food, shelter, health care, social relationship and education, within the context of a secure family life whether this be with natural parents or others;

(b) the means to develop a personal identity, self-respect, an awareness of their own worth and a sense of responsibility;

(c) the constancy of love, expressed through significant personal relationships;

(d) a secure base for a daily life and the opportunity to belong and be valued as a member of a community which offers an appropriate cultural environment;

(e) boundaries within which to grow and to develop self-discipline; and

(f) encouragement to be creative and to develop skills in order to realise their personal potential.

These rights, of course, apply to all children and therefore dictate the basic conditions for the boarding environment. They provide the framework within which the aims for boarding education can be developed. Further guidelines are to be found in *Homes are for Living in* (Social Services Inspectorate, 1989), in which basic values which underpin the quality of life for all children living in groups are summarised as: privacy, dignity, independence, choice, rights and fulfilment. While identifying the key values required specifically in a boarding environment, this list also provides an initial indication of aims.

The analysis prior to the formulation of boarding aims is carried a stage further in *The Children Act 1989, Guidance and Regulations, Volume 5 Independent Schools*:

> In safeguarding and promoting welfare, proprietors (and those to whom responsibility is delegated by them) need to be concerned with the health, happiness and proper physical, intellectual, emotional, social and behavioural development of that child, as well, of course, with protecting him against the risk of harm.

This statement sets out a baseline for the development of boarding aims, which can then be specified more fully in the light of the requirements for life in society, the accumulated wisdom of practitioners and other experts and the needs of the individual pupil.

The perceived needs for life in society provide a key source for the formulation of boarding aims. A detailed framework for these is given in *Personal and Social Education from 5 to 16* (Department of Education and Science, 1989). The inventory is divided into the familiar categories into which aims and objectives are normally classified. It should be stressed, however, that in using this analysis, aims and objectives should be formulated at levels appropriate to the ages and abilities of the pupils and that, within those constraints, each pupil develops at his own rate.

At the analysis stage, the other major source is the work of experts and practitioners. There are many books describing facets of boarding education, in particular, life in public schools, but the most complete piece of research remains that of Royston Lambert and his team, carried out in the 1960s. *A Manual to the Sociology of the School* (Lambert *et al.*, 1970) summarised the theory developed during the research and distinguished, for the boarding school, three kinds of goal: instrumental, expressive and organisational. These three were considered to provide a complete framework for the analysis of all school activities. Instrumental was defined as:

> that which is a means to a further end, that which appertains to performance in the sense of necessary technical operations rather than the satisfaction induced by performance or by attainment of the end of the performance.

Expressive was defined as that which is an end in itself (although it may have instrumental functions), that which satisfies the need disposition of the performer as distinct from the performance, the technical operations or processes necessary to attain such satisfaction. Organisational was defined as that which maintains an ongoing system. That the aims and objectives of boarding education can be subsumed within these three goals is evident from the breakdown of each provided. Instrumental goals consist of:

(a) academic, acquisition of knowledge, mental skills;
(b) vocational, preparation for job;
(c) personal and social training, manners, poise;
(d) training in being a competent citizen; and
(e) physical development and dexterity.

All of these, but particularly (b), (c) and (d) are directly related to personal and social development. The expressive goals were classified as:

(a) religious, pastoral care;
(b) ethical;
(c) cultural;
(d) personal development, creative expression; and

(e) sportsmanship.

Again, all can be seen as important in boarding education, but (d) is clearly a core area. Finally, organisational goals concern the machinery by which the society operates and are therefore less directly relevant. None the less, they include goals concerned with control, order and discipline, an important aspect of boarding education.

There are, of course, many such other inventories available, particularly in the field of life skills training and personal and social development in special schools, but these examples are sufficiently detailed to furnish a firm foundation for the analysis of material necessary to develop aims and objectives.

The formulation of aims and objectives

A detailed assessment of boarding education was made at Kenton Lodge School, Newcastle upon Tyne, between 1978 and 1981 (Anderson, 1979a, 1981). The children were of middle school age range and all had suffered some form of deprivation, so that there was a strong accent on compensatory personal and social education. The first stage in the development of aims was an analysis of the backgrounds and needs of the children. This revealed, for example, that there was a great need for stability, care, attention and affection. Using the work of Lambert and others, it was decided that deprivation could be classified into the following categories: personal, inter-personal, social, religious, moral and educational. Furthermore, it was thought that a distinction should be made between short-term aims (the period until the pupil leaves the school) and long-term aims (the school's contribution to the pupil's total education in fitting him to act with maturity in society). The same categories would obtain for both, but the long-term aims would be designed to fit the pupil for integration into society in terms of: domestic life, vocational life and recreational life.

With this background and framework, all members of staff, teaching and non-teaching, were asked to produce lists of what they considered to be important aims. The results were first categorised and then discussed in detail until agreement was reached. It was considered more important to identify key areas which would form the basis for aims, rather than to produce a set of terms which were mutually exclusive. For example, there can be some overlap between 'initiative' and 'flexibility', but they are none the less distinctive ideas with distinctive possibilities for monitoring. Indeed, in reality, the categories themselves are all closely interrelated in the development of the child and it is only for convenience and clarity that they are separated.

Since the framing of an aim, unlike that of an objective, does not involve any direct consideration of assessment, such elements as conditions and standards are not included in the statement. Therefore, rather than enter into what can well be repetitive and pedantic exercise, aims can be presented as a set of clearly defined topics. For personal and social development, the final list of aims, agreed at Kenton Lodge School was:

(a) personal: decision-making/accepting, independence, self-knowledge, self-discipline, initiative development of interests, leadership, good manners, care for self, flexibility, self-expression;

(b) inter-personal: care for others, ability to develop and sustain relationships, responsibility for others, co-operation, respect for others;

(c) social: respect for the needs of society as a whole, responsibility as a member within society, co-operation with society; and

(d) religious/moral: sound moral judgements and behaviour, respect for and obedience of the law, spiritual awareness.

Where appropriate, each of these aims was then broken down into its component objectives. For example, the breakdown of an aim on fitting children for community life in the school and in society, included the following topics, to be written later in objective form:

(a) manners at the table;
(b) smiles on greeting people;
(c) speaks to people in acceptable way;
(d) can talk on the telephone easily;
(e) shows pride in his appearance; and
(f) keeps his belongings tidy and clean.

Work from Kenton Lodge School is described in some detail, as it is the only example available which illustrates, for a boarding school, the complete procedure from the analysis through the formulation of aims and objectives to the assessment stage.

Although all the children at Kenton Lodge boarded as a result of social need, the school was not classified as 'special'. As a result of its small size Kenton Lodge facilitated a detailed case study and, in particular, an intensive assessment programme. The aims formulated are very much those which would be applicable in any residential school. Therefore it is felt that the procedure adopted at Kenton Lodge provides a model for use elsewhere.

In the boarding schools at large, an interest in the formulation of aims and objectives for boarding had been stimulated following the publication of *Boarding Education* 1 at the Boarding Schools Association housemasters' and housemistresses' conference in 1974. The next edition of *Boarding Education* contained an article on the subject (Anderson, 1975) in which the category, modes of personal operation, was introduced. As a result of discussions in some 20 boarding schools, a basic outline of aims which might be considered under personal development and community life, was produced.

Personal Development
Knowledge of the following areas:

(a) self, including own personal development and own motives and values;
(b) moral principles and values;
(c) Religious (or other) doctrine; and
(d) other people.

Skills:

(a) making sound moral judgements in school and in personal life;
(b) clarifying value issues in everyday situations; and
(c) working in creative way in personal life.

Attitudes:

(a) commitment to certain civilised values e.g. integrity, truth, justice, respect for persons;
(b) expectation of reflecting on personal experience and relating it to general principles;
(c) expectation of questioning assertions and checking facts; and
(d) expectation of maintaining physical fitness.

Modes of Personal Operation:

(a) receptiveness to the value commitments of others;
(b) creativeness in approaching personal questions of value;
(c) a habit of reflecting on first-hand experience and relating it to principle; and
(d) a habit of sensitiveness to the feelings and reactions of other individuals.

Community Life
Knowledge of the following areas:

(a) structure and organisation of the school and house, including consultation, innovation, etc;
(b) the variety of extra-curricular activities; and
(c) concept of an academic community with a religious component.

Skills:

(a) contributing to the organisation of activities;
(b) performance in a variety of extra-curricular activities; and
(c) performance as a member of a small group.

Attitudes:

(a) concern for harmony and vigour of school community;
(b) concern for welfare of neighbouring community;
(c) desire for effective collaboration with other people, whether congenial or not;
(d) willingness to throw self into life or school community and/or other community; and
(e) willingness to consider the bearing of religion on the life of the community.

Modes of Personal Operation:

(a) receptiveness to the ethos arising from the school's foundation;
(b) creativeness in building up and maintaining that ethos;
(c) a habit of reflecting on the community's life in the light of that ethos; and
(d) a habit of sensitiveness to the feelings and reactions of the community.

These aims were produced as illustrations of the different categories and levels which need to be examined. After further meetings, a loosely structured research programme was developed for the Boarding Schools Association. Stage one, in which house staff from 43 independent and maintained schools participated, consisted of an analysis of the boarding system. Diaries were kept of boarding activities on duty and non-duty nights and a list of all levels of contact between staff and pupils was maintained. As a result, a detailed picture of boarding activities was obtained for a wide range of schools and an analysis was made of the most complete data sets (Anderson, 1978).

Having discovered the basis of activities during boarding time, stage two was devoted to the formulation of aims and objectives, so that personal and social development could be more precisely monitored. Participants were asked to provide a list of the aims which fitted their particular perceptions of boarding and the results were classified in four categories.

(a) basic organisation: work, hygiene, punctuality, tidiness, getting clothes ready, planning generally, rule keeping, keeping quiet;
(b) self-development and attitudes: self-confidence, self-reliance, self-expression, talent to full, self-criticism, hobbies, self-caring, manners, morals;
(c) relationships: sharing attitude, tolerance and acceptance of others, control of aggression, ability to make friends, ability to talk to adults; and
(d) community: caring attitude, respect for others and property, live in a 'reasonable' way, show responsibility.

Since this list represents a summary of the thoughts of at least 43 practitioners, it obviously provides a useful guideline for the construction of aims. It covers the main areas subsumed under the title of personal and social development, together with a series of rather lower level aims, focusing on organisation.

Assessment

It is possible to obtain an overall impression of the personal and social development of a pupil, using a check list. If a grading system is applied, then changes over time can be noted and action, if necessary, taken. Such a check list was developed for boarding education at Wymondham College, Norfolk, the largest maintained boarding school in Europe. Apart from personal details, the following were checked termly:

(a) personal hygiene;
(b) experience of adventure;
(c) concern for standards in a non-sporting society;
(d) experience of non-academic success;
(e) attitude to study;
(f) development of philosophical interests;
(g) realistic awareness of own potential;
(h) affection given and taken;
(i) control of own feelings;
(j) sense of security;
(k) responsible initiative shown;
(l) appreciation of views of others;
(m) acceptance by peers of own sex;
(n) acceptance by peers of opposite sex;
(o) co-operation with staff;
(p) co-operation with peers; and
(q) understanding of this society's structure and social conventions.

This is a somewhat mixed list, including aims at different levels, but it does provide a very useful monitoring system. For the most part, it would also be applicable in a wide variety of residential schools.

The more structured formulation of aims can give a more precise assessment and can also facilitate the evaluation of the complete programme. This was achieved at Kenton Lodge School, using a variety of measures, the most direct of which was rating sheets. A five point scale was used to monitor the progress of the pupils towards the achievement of 11 key aims. Points one and five were carefully defined and all members of staff: care, teaching, clerical and domestic, were asked to score for each child with whom they had had any reasonable contact. The procedure was repeated at the end of each term and changes noted. One particularly interesting outcome was that, in the vast majority of cases, there was a close coincidence between the scores awarded, whichever staff group completed the form. The results from these forms provided the basis for the assessment of personal and social development, but were supplemented by information resulting from group work, incident sheets, counselling and observation. The aims, together with the definitions of behaviour at points one and five on each scale, are given below.

Aim	Rating 1	Rating 5
1. Self-discipline	lacks self-control, excessively noisy, panics easily	good control even in stressful conditions, can apply himself
2. Relationship with peers	always fighting, loner, not popular, no sympathy for peers, always arguing	good relationships, sympathy for others, highly supportive, respects others' needs
3. Relationship with adults	takes advantage of situations, not talkative	respects adults' needs, takes advice or guidance
4. Independence	needs support, cries at night, will not change clothes, cannot organise time	completely trustworthy, even caring for others, strong sense of security
5. Ability to accept valid decisions	always questions decisions, argues incessantly, defiant	discusses calmly, carries out decisions, can co-operate
6. Ability to share	very selfish, always takes largest helping, no interest in others	always shares food, will lend belongings freely
7. Care for self	always needs to be inspected, disregards own safety	careful, always neat, tidy, clean
8. Responsibility	constant supervision, totally irresponsible, cannot be trusted	can be left in charge, can make valid decisions, can organise and lead
9. Self-knowledge	no idea of limitations, little awareness of own feelings and actions	aware of own limitation, aware of own feelings and actions
10. Moral attitudes	bullies, cheats and lies, steals, unkind to others	considers others' needs and property
11. Good manners	no idea how to behave, table manners poor, completely thoughtless of comfort of others	well-mannered on all occasions

At Benton Grange School, Newcastle upon Tyne, a special school for girls, a more sophisticated procedure was developed, based on the work of Hunt and Sullivan (1974). The premiss is that all pupils pass through three conceptual levels:

(a) immature, unsocialised;
(b) dependent, conforming; and
(c) independent, self-reliant.

A particularly significant point is that it seems necessary to pass through the conforming stage before independence can be reached. The basic rating scales used at Kenton Lodge School could therefore be modified to take into account the three conceptual levels. Expected behaviour for each aim at each level was defined and this provided the basis for monitoring the personal and social development of the pupils. Once the conceptual level of an individual has been established, then not only will it be easier to forecast or understand behaviour in a particular situation, but appropriate rewards or punishments can be awarded. Furthermore, the level of the child also defines the most appropriate environment for development, from one which is highly structured to one which there is an emphasis on autonomy. The general characteristics, together with the behaviour for eleven key aims, is listed (p. 44). Once results have been obtained, using this method, it is possible to identify pupils more at risk and also develop more sophisticated measures for the boundaries. At Benton Grange School, the stages were each subdivided into sub-stages.

Conclusion

If boarding/residential education is thought to be a way of overcoming the problems of some children and of enhancing the personal and social development of others, it is essential that its effectiveness is measured. Aims and objectives which are carefully structured to facilitate monitoring procedures allow not only the assessment of individual performance, but an evaluation of the programme as a whole. Therefore, it is considered particularly worthwhile, when constructing a statement of principles for a boarding school, to include a series of carefully formulated aims for the non-classroom aspects of school life. Discussion on boarding aims is itself beneficial in that it ensures that all school practitioners are thinking in basically the same way and aiming in the same direction. More importantly, the statement of aims should provide the foundation on which the programme of boarding activities is based.

CHAPTER 4

Emotional and Developmental Welfare in the Light of the Children Act 1989

Suzanne Hutchinson

Introduction

The Children Act 1989 lays down detailed and comprehensive guidelines for the management of children in all residential environments, and a notable feature of the Act is the emphasis placed on ensuring and safeguarding the emotional and developmental welfare of such children. Thus in the case of children's homes it states:

> homes themselves must exercise the concern that a good parent would by providing a safe environment which promotes the child's development and protects him from exposure to harm in his contacts with other people or experiences in the community. (Guidance and Regulations Vol. 4: 1.1)

The guidance for independent schools is even more explicit:

> In safeguarding and promoting welfare, proprietors ... need to be concerned with the health, happiness, and proper physical, intellectual, emotional, social and behavioural development of that child, as well, of course, with protecting him against the risk of significant harm. (Guidance and Regulations Vol. 5: 2.4.1)

Furthermore, the Act requires from schools and other residential organisations a formal statement of aims and policies, and a well-documented structure for dealing with welfare issues with which all staff and others concerned with the care of the children are familiar. This is intended, presumably, to focus the minds of those running residential institutions on the precise nature and basis of their practices. There is a great diversity of approach and philosophy amongst different kinds of residential institution and even between individual institutions within the same category, and this creates difficulties in assessing the effectiveness of policy and practice within any one of them. What yardsticks should be used?

In some institutions, notably amongst boarding schools, the underlying ethos is powerful but has never been fully conceptualised, and may be based more firmly on traditional assumptions about children and child management than on clearly thought out principles implemented in a systematic way (Gathorne-Hardy, 1977; Walford, 1986). The Act requires a child-centred approach, designed to promote optimal development of the individual. It is likely that on close examination we would find the underlying aims of many schools and other institutions serving different ends, such as social control, the shaping of individuals to a preconceived standard, or the perpetuation of a moral or social system. In addition, over the years of an institution's existence, whatever the intentions of its founders, it can come to pass that organisational demands and staff convenience gradually take priority over children's needs. There is a strong case, therefore, for suggesting that all involved in residential care should examine carefully the true aims, stated or unstated, of their respective workplaces.

> The Act gives the opportunity to rethink practices and unless this is done there will be lost a rare and vital opportunity to improve the lot of children. (An Introduction to the Children Act 1989: 1.2)

There is a huge range of residential settings; boarding schools and schools which specialise in particular talents such as music or dance, residential homes for children taken into care, schools for children with behavioural difficulties and with other kinds of special needs, secure units for young offenders and children who constitute a serious threat to themselves or others. Is it possible that across this spectrum we can really identify common needs and common principles of practice?

I believe that we can, and should. There are certain basic needs that all children have, regardless of their background or special circumstances, if they are to achieve optimal development and stability in their emotional life and in their relationships. A clear understanding of these should be the basis of all childcare and management policies. We need to be aware of what happens when they are not met, or met only partially, and of how the damage can best be repaired. All children in residential settings are by definition separated for shorter or longer periods from their families. We need to understand how children react to separation, what causes the variations in response, and how to minimise the difficulties which can be raised by separation. This is relevant for the child abstracted from a grossly deficient environment, for the child at boarding school who is there through personal or parental choice, and for all shades of need or compulsion in between. Once these general principles are agreed, it becomes possible to apply them systematically to specific settings, and to develop the appropriate emphases, organisational structures, staff skills and environmental characteristics needed by the children who are served by them.

Until Freud made his startling claim that what happened early in life had significant implications for later mental health and social functioning, little attention had been paid to exactly how the human personality is constructed. He and his followers based their theories about child development, which were revolutionary in their time, on information gained through their work with the dysfunctional adults they treated in their clinics, by a process of retrospective deduction. Field-studies carried out during the 1940s by Anna Freud and her associates, on young children who were separated from their families, caused a quieter revolution in the way in which child development was researched. In 1950, John Bowlby was asked by the World Health Organization to investigate the mental health of homeless children. The resulting report (Bowlby, 1951) became the inspiration for a great deal of further work which took the actual behaviour of babies and children as the starting-point. There is now a substantial and well-established body of knowledge about the processes of human emotional and cognitive development.

It is beyond the scope of this chapter to review comprehensively the enormous literature on child psychology and welfare which has been generated during the last 50 years. The point is that it exists, and we have no legitimate excuse, as active agents in the care and welfare of children, for ignoring its messages. In the next section I shall summarise what I believe to be the basic needs of all children, whatever their backgrounds, and whatever the aims of the residential establishments in which they find themselves.

Developmental needs of children

The ideal scenario

Jenny is a much-wanted baby who experiences a quick, easy birth following trouble-free foetal development. She is born into a family which has planned carefully for her arrival. Her mother is well supported by her husband and family during the early weeks, so that she can concentrate fully on her baby's needs. Jenny is fed when she is hungry, comforted when she is frightened, changed when she is wet or uncomfortable, and her earliest attempts to gain a response from her environment are met happily by her mother and father. By about six months, she is showing quite clearly the ability to differentiate between people, and has a marked preference for her mother, to whom she always turns first when she is distressed. She discovers that Mother does not always respond instantly to her needs any more, and that this is not the end of the world.

Over the next few years she learns gradually and gently the limits of her influence over the other people in her life. This is quite considerable, as they are always respectful of her needs and wishes, even if they do not always decide to accede to them. She is encouraged to practise her ever-growing compendium of skills and abilities, and when it is all too much to handle, Mother or Father are always there to run back to. When she succeeds in anything, however small, the appropriate praise and encouragement are forthcoming in generous measure. By this time Jenny is a contented, energetic and inquisitive toddler who relates well to most people. Round about now there is a new baby in the family. While Mother is in hospital, Jenny is cared for in her own home by other members of the family whom she has known all her life, and she visits her mother and the new baby daily. Her own position in the family is constantly reaffirmed, and therefore even when her mother is immersed in caring for the baby, Jenny does not feel superceded. In due course, it is time for her to go to school. It is a major transition in her life, and the family celebrates it accordingly.

Life is tougher and more challenging now, but she knows that at home there is constant love and support where she can recharge her batteries. She enjoys learning, takes á pride in doing well, and when things go wrong it does not dent her confidence because she has a realistic sense of her own worth. Jenny is now a child with well-developed self-esteem, secure in her important relationships. Her attitude to life and other people is positive. She has a strong sense of agency, that who she is and what she does counts in her world, even if other people sometimes count more. Jenny is in a good position to tackle adolescence, separation from the family, new and more testing life experiences, intimate relationships, and adulthood. Most important of all, her positive expectations of life are likely to be self-fulfilling.

The 'good enough' environment

It is not impossible for there to be children as lucky as Jenny, but more often than not, even in the most caring of families, life does not run that smoothly. External events may preclude the consistent parental presence and support Jenny enjoyed. Parental problems of ill-health, poor relationships, poverty or isolation can leave insufficient energy for dealing patiently with a small child. Many families have full-time working parents, or parents who are frequently either away from home or so immersed in their work that they have little time for their children. D.W. Winnicott's concept of the 'good enough' parent came as something of a relief against a background of mounting evidence of the importance of early life experiences in the mental health of the individual. It seemed that parents, however hard they tried, could never get it quite right. He came to the conclusion that as long as children received just enough of the kind of attention and care they needed to build an adequate self-image and hold a reasonably hopeful view of life, they would grow into autonomous adults capable of good-quality relationships.

Basic developmental requirements of children

a) A safe haven
The most important requirement for healthy development is a place of safety where a child can receive support and nurturing. It is every child's right to have parents or other caretakers who

actively seek to protect her from harm and support her in times of stress, and a helpful environment in which to grow.

This most basic of rights is fundamental to the thinking behind the Children Act, from the detailed guidelines for Care Orders to the repeated emphasis on the paramountcy of the welfare of the child in all circumstances.

It is easy to comprehend the effects of material deprivation and physical abuse, but the effects of emotional deprivation and abuse are just as devastating and in some ways even more dangerous because they can be so subtle and so difficult to diagnose. A child whose material situation is good and who appears to have everything he could wish for may find it impossible to understand the unhappiness he experiences, because he has no way of discerning how poorly his emotional needs are met within his family. His unhappiness is compounded by guilt and confusion. The people around him also find it hard to perceive the source of his anxieties, and assume that the trouble lies within him rather than being the result of his experiences. Equally, the emotional impact of physical and sexual abuse is often underestimated or poorly understood, and indeed even now the legal processes to which children who have been abused are sometimes subjected demonstrate a lamentable lack of comprehension of the emotional trauma suffered by the victim.

b) Recognition as an individual

> Homes should set out to treat each child as an individual person.
> (Guidance and Regulations Vol. 4: 1.1)

Every human being needs to be recognised by those close to him as uniquely and valuably himself. In caring families, whatever problems there might be, each member knows that he or she has a place that could not be filled by any other person. There are many ways in which this basic need can be thwarted. If the family's circumstances are very difficult, the parents may have no energy or will to treat their children as individuals — they are overstretched just coping with their own problems. Sometimes parents see in a child the potential they themselves were unable to develop through lack of opportunity, and the child becomes the vehicle for their own unrealised ambitions, her particular talents and her wishes ignored. An unhappy parent can come to rely on a child for emotional and practical support, where the strength of the parent's needs precludes his recognition of his child as a person with needs of his own. A parent who herself suffered that kind of upbringing, where the boundaries between the generations were not respected, would find it difficult to experience her child as separate from herself, and would assume that the child thought and felt exactly as she did.

Children who have not had their need for recognition met with sufficient consistency lack a clear sense of self and have poor self-esteem. They are ill-equipped to form good interpersonal relationships, cope confidently with life-problems, or withstand stress. Some use attention-seeking behaviour in an effort to force people to see them, others blend in with the scenery, the docile, undemanding children whom no-one really notices. There can be an intense sense of hopelessness and worthlessness, even of self-hatred. Frequently when these children grow up they enter relationships in which they are emotionally or sexually exploited.

c) Affirmation of thoughts and feelings

This is closely related to the point above in that the most effective way of denying individuality is to disconfirm the thoughts or feelings of the individual. The kind of intensity of children's emotions are often painful or inconvenient for the adults around them. 'It doesn't really matter', we say to a child who is bitterly disappointed because he did not make the football team. 'You know Mummy and Daddy love each other really', accords ill with he constant rguments and slammed doors the child experiences day by day. Some children are subjected to such constant disconfirmations of their feelings and experiences that they grow up doubting their inner reality. An extreme form of this, well-ocumented by R.D. Laing (1961, 1964) is the powerful family-system to which every member is expected to conform. Any ideas or feelings which do not fit into the system are ruthlessly suppressed.

Children who suffer constant disconfirmation of their feelings grow up with a sense of unreality and confusion. They repress the unacceptable feelings, often to such an extent that they no longer have access to them. They school themselves to 'feel' only what the significant others in their lives find acceptable. They develop what Winnicott called the 'false self', a mask with which the child identifies wholly, leaving the real person hidden and condemned. Laing believed this kind of experience to be, in its extreme form, a major contributory factor in mental illnesses such as schizophrenia.

d) Consistent parenting

Children need their parents or caretakers to give them consistent messages so that they can gain some sense of order and coherence in their lives. If parents are reliable in their actions and reactions, there is a comforting element of predictability in life which is a major source of personal security. In contrast, the emotionally volatile mother who shouts at her son one minute and cuddles him the next, the father whose rules seem to change every day and whose rewards and punishments seem equally incomprehensible, the family-system which is covertly organised around the arbitrary demands of its most powerful member, parents who strongly condemn behaviour in their children to which they then subject the children themselves, are all examples of inconsistency of approach which can be very damaging to a child.

Such children live with the certainty that nothing they do is ever right, that however hard they try they will never succeed in pleasing, and that they have no control over their lives. They develop 'antennae' by which they seek to assess the reactions of powerful others, so that they can try to guess correctly what they will do next. Their self-esteem is low, and they find it very difficult to trust other people in later life.

e) Warm, appropriate (non-sexual) physical contact

Babies need an enormous amount of physical contact in their early days. Without it, they fail to thrive and may even die. This fact has become relatively well understood. What is perhaps less well understood is that the need for close, accepting contact with other human bodies does not diminish as children grow up. They may need it less frequently — but no less intensely. There is much that can get in the way of this most simple of human needs. Fashions in child-raising have at times dictated that too much cuddling is bad for children and risks spoiling them; that babies who cry for no apparent reason are being naughty and should be left; that physical comfort for a distressed child can undermine his growth towards independence; and that children, boys in particular, should learn as soon as possible to be brave, independent and tough. Another set of barriers is created, especially in fathers, by modern concerns about the nature of touching and contact, and fears about appropriateness. And for some parents, who perhaps received little physical contact during their own childhoods, or who have other emotional or psychological problems, cuddling their children does not come easily and may even seem impossible.

Physical contact is so important in establishing a child's sense of acceptability and security that lack of it can have a wide variety of more or less unhappy effects. These effects are less severe if most of the other basic needs are adequately met, but even in the most stable and well-balanced personality there can be a deep longing, and fear of ultimate unacceptability, which can be traced back to a childhood starved of hugs.

Perhaps a measure of its importance is the enormity of the damage that can be done when a child's need for contact is abused. Perhaps the saddest thing of all is that a child will settle for abusive contact rather than have none at all.

f) Praise and encouragement

> [Care staff] should recognise and applaud a young person's achievements and encourage him to take pride in his successes. (Guidance and Regulations Vol. 4: 1.107)

From their earliest years, and throughout childhood and adolescence, children need to be praised for their achievements, however small, and encouraged to try new experiences, take age-appropriate risks, and discover and develop their individual skills and strengths. In that way they gain solid self-esteem and confidence in their ability to tackle new experiences and solve problems successfully. They are also much more likely to learn in a way that does not threaten their positive self-image just what their personal limitations are.

Children for whom praise and encouragement are not forthcoming are likely to come to the conclusion that nothing they do has any value or significance – that they are not good enough. Some may accept this verdict and go on to fulfil it whilst others spend their lives trying to prove to themselves and others that it is not true, with every success discounted and every failure magnified.

g) Belonging
Every human being has a deep-rooted need to belong to a group with which he can identify himself and within which he has a recognisable role. The primary group is the family, but the search

for group identity extends further as the child grows older, towards social, cultural and national membership. The significance of group membership for personal identity and self-image should never be underestimated (Brown, 1988). One of the most frightening and dehumanising conditions for any human being is that of isolate or outcast. In addition, the major life transitions tend to be marked by the movement from one social grouping to another, and at critical times membership of a particular group can provide the safety and stability needed by the individual to complete the transition successfully. The importance of the peer-group during adolescence is an example of this.

A crucial factor in the ability of an individual to form group relationships successfully is the experience he or she had of being accepted and valued within the family group. Many children suffer from an indefinable but immensely painful feeling of 'being on the outside looking in', and however hard they try, and however successful they appear to an outsider to be, never feel that they really 'belong'. This feeling accompanies them throughout their adult lives. Another cause of this kind of suffering is that of dislocation from one familial, cultural, social or national group to another, and this is a point of special significance for those running residential establishments. The significance for the individual of adequate group relationships is explored by Martin Callow in Chapter 7.

The effect of the residential environment

Children who have 'good enough' experiences of having these basic needs met will generally be able to deal successfully with the pressures of community life – so long as the community offers them a reasonable continuation of their positive experiences. If it does not, then even the best-adjusted child is likely to have difficulties. We tend to focus on the child, or blame the family, when problems arise whilst he is resident with us. In fact it may well be that the environment we provide is causing that child such stress that his perfectly healthy coping mechanisms break down.

Case study 1
Emma decided to go to boarding school for her two years in the sixth-form. She was a quiet girl, but did not lack for confidence and knew that she had the necessary academic ability to do well. She looked forward to making new friends and to taking part in

the many activities available. Her family were supportive of her decision, making it clear that they would miss her during term-time but that they respected her wish to gain a measure of independence before going to college.

The boarding house in which Emma found herself was run largely by the senior girls, as the Housemistress believed that they should be given the opportunity of exercising responsibility and authority. Normally this arrangement worked well, but Emma happened to come at a time when the senior year-group included two girls who delighted in making the lives of the newcomers a misery in many small, spiteful ways. For some reason, they picked on Emma as their favourite target, shaming her in front of the other girls, hiding books and notes so that she got into trouble with some of the teachers, spreading rumours about her which made it difficult for her to make friends elsewhere in the school. Eventually in desperation she asked to speak to the Housemistress, who after listening to her story, with its many apparently insignificant grievances, reassured her that boarding for the first time was often difficult but that a positive approach would overcome the problems. She implied, in the kindest way, that Emma was making mountains out of molehills and told her that the first step towards independence was learning to fight one's own battles.

Emma was too ashamed to ask for help again, or to burden her family with her problems when it had been her idea to board in the first place. She began to sleep badly, her appetite failed, she found her work increasingly difficult, and she became withdrawn and uncommunicative. A teacher drew the attention of the Housemistress to her state, and she was sent to the school doctor. He diagnosed depression and prescribed anti-depressant tablets. The Housemistress concluded that Emma was a weak character who should not have come to boarding school.

In many cases, the children who are cared for in residential establishments have not had uniformly helpful life-experiences, and enter the community damaged in some way. They may have behavioural difficulties of greater or lesser severity, and difficulties in forming healthy relationships with peers or adults. For these children, the provision of the kind of help and attention they need so badly starts with a helpful and supportive environment, even though much more than that may be required.

Case study 2

David was taken into care at the age of ten. When he appeared at the Home he was undersized, poorly dressed and still covered with weals where his father had taken his belt to him. He was nervous, suspicious and aggressive towards the other children. After a few days it was noticed that he had attached himself to a young care assistant and was following her unobtrusively around the house. She was encouraged to engage him in casual conversation whenever she found a suitable opportunity, and gradually he began to respond. She encouraged him to talk about himself, paying careful attention. He said she reminded him of his older sister, who had left home the previous year.

In the case discussion meetings the staff planned how to marshall the kind of support David needed within the orderly routine of the home with its high tolerance of disturbed behaviour. Particular attention was paid to his relationships with the other children, and low-key intervention by staff in tense situations enabled David to relax his attitude of wary belligerence and take part more readily in social activities. In due course, when it was believed that he felt secure enough in his new environment to cope with it, he was engaged in regular sessions with the consultant psychologist who began the long, painful task of unmasking and attempting to heal the damage that had been done.

It is not only to establishments designed to cater for them that damaged children come. Boarding schools do not, except for a notable few, have as their main aim the care of children with emotional problems. However, deprivation and abuse are not confined to that section of the population commonly described as underprivileged, but occur across the whole of the social spectrum. A glance at the statistics suggests that between 5 per cent and 10 per cent of boarding pupils are likely to present with problems of some severity during their school careers. Perhaps 1 per cent are likely to be extremely serious. Provided that the environment is good enough, and that good enough attention is paid to all individuals within the school, these problems will get picked up. Every school needs to have in place the necessary structures to deal with them.

Attributes of a helpful residential environment

When children arrive in a residential institution with problems already entrenched, their new environment can confirm their view of life, make it even worse, or provide a situation in which some attempt at solutions and healing can be made. For children who do not arrive with problems, the majority in the case of boarding schools, the environment can sometimes, as I have illustrated, create them. Alternatively it can have a neutral effect. The best outcome is that it genuinely enhances the experiences of the pupils and offers them opportunities for further development. In terms of the relationship between staff and children problems are created or helped in residential settings through three media; organisation, ethos and relationships. The physical environment is also extremely important and a later chapter in this book is devoted to it.

Organisation

All communities have some practical considerations to address in the way they are planned and managed. There is generally a financial constraint, there are likely to be physical constraints in the shape of buildings and facilities, and there are almost invariably those outside the institution who have a powerful say in how it is organised. In addition, there are all the inescapable details of enabling a community to function efficiently, in terms of routine, discipline, timetabling and use of facilities. It is not surprising that sometimes the compromises that have to be made between the needs of the individual and those of the organisation favour the latter. One might go so far as to say that, unless a regular check upon the community's priorities is built into the structure, organisational convenience is likely to take over, slowly and steadily, even in the most caring of institutions. The Act requires that institutions which care for children on a residential basis be organised, or re-organised, in a child-centred manner. That is, the welfare of the children has to take priority at all times over all other considerations.

This means that those with managerial responsibility have to consider carefully just what their processes and structures are intended to achieve, and whether the needs of the children in their care are best served by just those methods. For example, it may be organisationally convenient to prevent children visiting the nearby town, a source of alcohol and cigarettes and occasionally of behaviour embarrassing to the institution. But, other than those who are confined for a reason, children should have contact with the world outside the institution, and so the organisation must find ways of dealing with the unacceptable consequences other than banning or restricting access. Likewise, although it is easier to supervise a large group of children if they are all in one place, it may not be in the best interests of the younger children to be mixed in with older ones. Even purely administrative functions can have unhelpful effects and need to be scrutinised. The way letters are handed out, for instance, can highlight the child who never receives any mail, and when a cafeteria system is used rather than one in which each child sits at an allotted table, mealtimes can be purgatory for children who are unpopular or isolated for any reason.

Staff roles: the need for clarity and structure

Children feel more secure in an environment where those who deal with them have clearly defined roles and act consistently within them. This is true in families; many studies have confirmed that behavioural and emotional problems arise when there are no clear boundaries between the parents or caretakers and their children, or when the adults of the family act in a way which is inconsistent with their adult status and responsibilities. It is equally true in institutions. Adults who cross over the boundaries, who try to identify with the children in order to be accepted by them, at best lose the respect of those in their charge and at worst can fall into inappropriate and damaging emotional relationships. Carers whose fulfilment of their role is inconsistent, or who are unpredictable in the way they relate to the children, cause anxiety to the children who therefore cannot develop trusting relationships with them.

As well as consistency of approach, staff need to demonstrate the existence of a supportive and dependable structure in the daily life of the institution. Routine may be frustrating at times, but lack of it creates anxiety. This is particularly true for younger children, and for those of any age who have suffered from lack of stability and order in their lives. There are many children from materially comfortable backgrounds whose family circumstances do not allow for order and routine, so that this factor is just as important in the boarding house as it is in the establishment which caters for the underprivileged or abused. It is worth noting that although children in a boarding house are inevitably subject to the whole-school routine, and may thus be thought to have their needs for structure met through the school, if the boarding house itself does not have a sufficiently supportive structure its less secure members will still suffer high levels of anxiety, and may also find it difficult to organise the parts of their lives which take place outside the boarding house.

Routine and structure are also helpful to the new member of a residential community in that they enable him to grasp the essential elements of the environment sooner rather than later. The degree of familiarity which the child feels with the environment is a significant factor in creating or minimising stress:

> New and especially challenging environments present a person with a period of low environmental control: new faces, places, routines and rules have to be assimilated.... Loss of control over the environment is increasingly recognised as a source of stress. (Fisher, 1991)

Care staff can do much to ameliorate this aspect of newness through the way in which they structure the child's first days and weeks. Information about the rules and routines should be readily accessible, and induction activities need to be designed to familiarise him as rapidly as possible with all aspects of daily life in the community. If there are one or two key staff who make a point of learning his name and circumstances from the day he arrives, who take positive steps to check on his progress, and who make it plain to him that he is welcome to turn to them for practical information and guidance, he will quickly gain confidence in his dealings with the system and the other adults in it. A child who is faced with a number of people all of whom appear to have claims on his attention and none of whom seem particularly approachable is much more vulnerable to feelings of powerlessness and confusion.

Age-appropriate regimes

Young children need a well-regulated regime with a great deal of adult attention and intervention. As they get older, children need less practical attention from carers. Their emotional needs do not diminish, though they change. The respect of their carers enhances their sense of agency and self-worth, and the opportunity to exercise greater levels of responsibility and autonomy, within an environment which tolerates mistakes and enables them to pick up the pieces of personal disasters, becomes increasingly important. In some ways working with adolescents demands even greater sensitivity and flexibility than working with younger children, because the lines between firmness and repression, emotional support and intrusiveness, tolerance and apparent indifference, are so finely drawn. The most complex environments are those which cater for a wide age-range, for it is very difficult to provide enough support and protection for the youngest and enough freedom for the oldest. It is also difficult for staff to adapt their approaches on a minute-by-minute basis! Perhaps the most important thing to bear in mind is that reasonably well-balanced older children can tolerate quite high levels of environmental stress whereas very young children, and those whose emotional development has been impaired, can not.

Keeping in touch with the outside world

> The importance of being able to get to the schools, shops, youth clubs and other facilities in the community cannot be overestimated. (Guidance and Regulations Vol. 4: 1.58)

Life in a residential community can be very intense and inward-looking, particularly when education and leisure facilities are all located on site. It might be considered, for instance, that children at boarding schools have free access to 'the outside world' during vacations, and that therefore confinement during term-time to the school grounds except for limited access to nearby towns or villages is not likely to cause problems. It can and does. The lack of privacy and the difficulty of finding personal space in community living create anxiety and stress for many children which freedom to leave the school site alleviates considerably. School trips may have interest or cultural value, but do not replace the freedom to choose when and where to go in leisure time. Naturally there are constraints of organisation and safety to be considered, but all schools should examine whether their policies on this matter present the best possible compromise from the pupils' point of view. Those living in children's homes generally attend local schools, and the guidelines stress that they should be encouraged to establish links within the local community, and to pursue friendships made at school: 'It is also important to recognise the value of peer group relationships made in educational settings (Guidance and Regulations Vol. 4: 2.33).

In situations where the children are unable, whether through disability or for other reasons, to leave the site informally, it becomes particularly important to organise excursions which bring them into contact with people outside the institution and offer opportunities for activities and experiences beyond those which the institution can provide. In most instances the value of the different perspectives gained from integration in the everyday world beyond the gates outweighs the organisational problems and inconveniences.

Complaints procedures: giving children a voice

In every institution, however carefully and caringly it is run, there is always the possibility that there will be individuals who become victims of bullying or scapegoating, or who are drawn into inappropriate relationships with other children or irresponsible members of the staff. In well-run institutions there are many adults to whom a child can safely turn, but if he is severely depressed, or if he has little trust in authority figures, he may not feel able to approach them. The Act states that in all residential institutions, whatever their purpose, there must be a well-publicised complaints procedure which a child can access easily (Guidance and Regulations Vol. 4 Ch. 5; Vol. 5: 3.11.1). The procedure must make plain the hierarchy of responsibility within the institution, and most importantly it must include the facility to make contact outside it as well. Every child must be taught who he can go to and how to set about it, and every member of staff must have a clear knowledge of the extent and limits of their responsibilities with regard to complaints.

The objective is plain enough; to safeguard against every eventuality the welfare of children. Fears have been expressed that publicising a procedure such as this will lead to abuse of it by children with mischievous motives. The experience gained from Childline suggests that this will not occur often enough to invalidate the directive as a valuable safety-net. The enormous number of calls received by Childline, many of which concerned problems of considerable severity, highlighted the need for a safe recourse for children independent of the significant adults in their lives. In the six months during which a Boarding School Line was in operation, there were approximately 10,000 calls, 1,000 of which resulted in some kind of counselling. While only 1 per cent of boarders who used the line required active help, the fact that 9,000 other children found occasion to use the line demonstrates a need for someone to talk to, perhaps about quite trivial concerns, who is outside the institution and even outside the family.

In my opinion the directive holds great significance for children. It provides a clear message that their interests are regarded as paramount, and that they are not condemned to be helpless in the hands of more powerful others. It gives them the possibility of exercising a degree of control over what happens to them, and that is extremely important. I feel therefore that, far from playing down the existence of the procedure, as some institutions might be tempted to do, it should be emphasised to children that they do have this escape route, this degree of control over their lives, if they should ever find themselves in need of it. Certainly the chances are that complaints will be made more frequently, and that not all of them will be justified, but that should not be seen as a problem. When a complaint is made, it gives the institution the chance to put right anything that is wrong − for we are, are we not, attempting to give the very best of care at all times − or alternatively to explain to the complainant why his or her complaint is inappropriate. It has been suggested that it will not be the homes or schools from which many complaints proceed that will give cause for greatest concern, but rather those from which no complaints proceed, for that will indicate that the procedures for making complaints either do not exist or are not working!

Useful outsiders

a) Special provisions
Establishments whose *raison d'être* is the treatment of disturbed children have, or should have, available to them as a matter of course a team of child guidance professionals to supplement their own staff skills. What is perhaps less well recognised is that all institutions which care for children should have access to such people, for even in the most 'normal' population there are certain to be individuals who present problems which are beyond the competence of the care staff to handle. The Social Services now have a duty to make child guidance services available to all children, even those in private education who in the past were often regarded as having opted out of the state welfare system. The route to these services usually lies through the General Practice which has taken on medical responsibility for the institution, but some boarding schools have recognised the value of setting up their own support

service, sometimes with an in-house counsellor, sometimes with an external professional who agrees to offer a specified range of services which may include staff support and consultation as well as referral of children. Ideally, children should have free access to a counsellor without staff having to know about it, though this can be difficult to achieve. In other sectors, there is a move towards sending specific members of staff for intensive training, so that they can bring back new knowledge and skills to pass on to the other staff in the organisation, and this is seen as a more satisfactory and more cost-effective method of gaining increased professional expertise within the organisation.

b) Other staff within the organisation
Another source of help for children distinct from the staff who have pastoral responsibilities for them may be people who work at the institution in other capacities. Medical staff are frequently approached by children who need to talk confidentially with someone. More problematically, anyone who works on site in a capacity which brings him of her into possible contact with the children may be used in the same way. The value of this lies in the increased range of adult contacts, particularly non-authoritarian adult contacts, that children have available to them (see Martin Callow, Chapter 7), but there is a risk that such people might not always be able to deal appropriately with everything that comes their way. The Act recognises this possibility through its insistence that all proprietors take every precaution against employing anyone, in any capacity, who is known to be unfit to work with children, and it stresses that all employees who have potential contact with children need to know what the welfare procedures are and where their responsibilities begin and end (Guidance and Regulations Vol. 4: 1.34; Vol. 5: 3.3.1). This is a tall order in a large establishment such as a boarding school, with employee numbers in the hundreds, and a high turnover of casual staff! In such cases vigilance on the part of care staff and management is the best defence.

Ethos

The ethos of a school or home has a powerful influence on the group behaviour and expectations of both staff and children, and will dictate whether or not the environment is essentially helpful. We need to study the nature of the formal code which governs the official relationships between members of the care staff and the children, and whether this is coherent and clearly stated, as the Act now requires, or largely implicit and open to individual interpretation. Do the staff as a group work within it, or is there instead a great variation in staff attitudes and responses? Unthinking and inflexible adherence to a code is of course as dangerous as the absence of any coherent set of aims and principles; a balance has to be achieved between the need for consistency and for sufficient flexibility to adjust the system when it is deemed appropriate. We also need to look at the prevailing group ethos amongst the children, and whether it runs parallel with, or counter to, the official ethos. How rigid or flexible is the peer-group culture, and how strong is the pressure to conform to it?

It might be supposed that the ideal situation would comprise a staff group whose personal approaches coincided with the formal ethos of the establishment, and a child group which readily conformed to it. Certainly, if there is too great a deviation in either group from an acceptable norm, then the community and/or the individual is placed under stress, but a degree of tension between individuals and the organisation, and between groups and subgroups, is healthy and gives rise to opportunities for personal and social exploration and development (Kahan, 1988). For example, a strong peer-group culture which is clearly differentiated from the formal ethos without being in direct conflict with it may provide valuable support for a child who is struggling to find a sense of identity and autonomy; and a willingness on the part of staff to question the status quo and to experiment − within reason − with different ways of handling their various tasks is the best prophylactic against organisational rigidity and the possibility of abuse.

Relationships

The quality of the experience of a child in a residential setting is crucially affected by the quality of the relationships he is able to sustain with both staff and peers, and ultimately, successful personal and social development hinges upon the ability to form satisfactory personal relationships. It is thus important to look closely at the ways in which these relationships are framed and the pressures to which they are subjected. We need to understand the ways in which people protect themselves on the one hand and attempt to get their needs met on the other. It cannot be stressed too heavily that this applies as much to staff as it does to children. We need then to ask whether and how the formal community contains and responds to these personal needs and expectations of its members, and how it deals with the defences. The guidelines to the Act are explicit about the importance of appropriately warm and supportive relationships between staff and the children in their care. For example, in the case of boarding house staff:

> Staff relationships with boarders cannot replicate those to be found in a good family but they must be warm and supportive, and capable of celebrating achievement, providing support, anticipating problems and dealing with disciplinary matters sensibly and fairly. (Department of Health, *The Welfare of Children in Boarding Schools: Practice Guide* 6.42)

For both boarding pupils and children in residential care good quality relationships between staff and children are seen as the basis of good discipline:

> A major determinant of good behaviour and positive ethos of the home is the quality of the relationships between the staff and the children. (Guidance and Regulations Vol. 4: 1.85)

> [Factors which create a successful and well-disciplined atmosphere include] . . . the quality of relationships between boarders and staff. There needs to be a mutual respect and understanding between boarders and staff. (Guidance and Regulations Vol. 5: 3.9.2)

This is most certainly a correct approach. Children are not in general unaware of the necessity for discipline; for example, in a questionnaire survey of pupil attitudes in a boarding school an overwhelming majority agreed with the statement 'It is necessary to have quite strict rules in a boarding school' (Hutchinson, 1991). However, they are much more amenable to it if they are given a clear rationale by staff who respect them sufficiently to take the trouble to explain the basis of any disciplinary proceedings, and who are known to be fair in their application of them. Staff whose relationships with children are not based on mutual respect tend to rely more heavily on formal disciplinary processes than those whose approach to the children in their care is positive, friendly and firm.

The residential aspects of the institution can be framed in such a way as to encourage and enhance positive and constructive relationships between the children as well. Unobtrusive but close observation will enable timely low-key interventions in tense situations and more forceful interventions when necessary. Flexible rooming arrangements mean that children who do not relate well to each other can be separated and placed with more congenial room-mates. When children's interests are actively engaged on behalf of a struggling contemporary, a seam of supportive concern can be mined which, handled sensitively, can provide just the affirmation and sense of personal value needed to shore up a faltering ego. Even in some more serious cases peer-group understanding and tolerance can enable the problematic individual to work through his difficulties within the community rather than having to leave it. Above all, consistency of approach and obvious fairness provide the necessary security for children to relax with the staff and each other sufficiently for good-quality relationships to be fostered.

Maintenance of family relationships

> the Children Act imposes a new duty to promote contact between a child who is being looked after ... and those who are connected with him. These people include the child's parents, any one else with parental responsibility for him and any relative or friend of the child, unless it is not reasonably practicable or consistent with the child's welfare to do so. (Guidance and Regulations Vol. 4: 4.6)

John Bowlby and the many researchers who followed his lead discovered that the single most important factor in a child's successful adaptation to separation from the family was maintenance of contact with family members. Also, children who had siblings with them in the new setting suffered less than those who were separated from them. There are unfortunate children who are being separated from their families for very good reasons, but even then, if there is any relative or even friend of the family with whom a child has some kind of positive relationship, then contact with such a person helps to preserve a degree of continuity in the child's experience. It is particularly important in the early days of separation, such as the first few weeks at boarding school, that children should feel that their families are freely accessible, even if it is only through letters or telephone calls. It is also important that crying or other displays of distress are not discouraged, either by the staff or by other children, for they provide necessary relief from painful feelings and emotional tension. Much of the damage suffered by children as a result of separation from their families arises precisely because they are forced to suppress and deny their emotions.

Parents often worry when they receive daily tearful calls from their offspring. Although occasionally a child fails to settle, in general, if homesickness is well handled by staff, after a few days or weeks the adaptation is made and the child or adolescent goes on to enjoy the new experiences to be found in community living. What is happening during those early days is that the child, whatever her age, is under serious stress and is reverting to early attachment behaviour in order to elicit the needed reassurance and support. As long as it is forthcoming from her family, and they are firm in their encouragement of her new venture and their faith in her ability to cope, she will settle sooner rather than later. If this kind of support is not available from her family, then coping is very much harder and she will need a great deal of sensitive attention from the staff who care for her. It is easy to underestimate the enormity of the culture-shock many children experience when they first enter residential institutions. Those who adapt readily are no more the norm than those who do not. Maintaining healthy family relationships is the single most important ingredient in going on to develop and sustain good-quality relationships in the new environment.

In this context it is worth noting that parents are not always well prepared for separation from their offspring. Boarding schools could and probably should do a great deal more to make sure that 'first-time buyers', those who have no previous experience of boarding either for themselves or for their children, understand both the practicalities and the emotional implications of their decision to allow their children to board. When a child is taken into care, it is necessary for parents or others who have close emotional ties with the child to be given as much information as possible about what will be happening for the child. Perhaps most importantly, whatever the reason for the separation, parents should be advised about how children commonly react to new environments and the reasons for the reactions. At the same time they should have clear information about how the establishment handles the problems of adaptation that children sometimes display.

To sum up, it is possible to organise and structure the residential experience in such a way that the children are given the best possible chance of finding everything they need for their emotional and developmental welfare, whilst receiving maximum protection from harm. What of the staff who have this enormous responsibility placed on their shoulders?

Good care staff: born not made?

The routes into pastoral work in residential settings are heavily dependent on the nature of the institutions, which means that people enter it from a variety of backgrounds and with considerable variations in training. Particularly in specialist institutions offering treatment and psychotherapy, staff may be extremely highly trained. Others may have had social work or youth work training, or have medical qualifications. Some have had minimal training of any kind, and in the report of the Independent Review of Residential Care chaired by Gillian Wagner, published in 1988, comment is made about 'the lack of training and of knowledge about the philosophy of residential work or of what constitutes good or bad practice', resulting in low esteem and low morale. In boarding schools, it is still rare for staff to have had any kind of formal training for pastoral work; they have traditionally been expected to learn as they go along. In a minority of schools, more frequently single-sex girls' schools or preparatory schools, the boarding houses are run by non-teaching staff, who in some instances have low status and influence compared with teaching staff, but in most senior schools all or most teaching staff are expected to fulfil a pastoral role, and housemasters or housemistresses teach anything from half to a full timetable. Many schools employ in addition full- or part-time matrons who may have nursing qualifications but who are infrequently given any specific training for pastoral work.

How, then, do people with pastoral responsibilities manage to fulfil them adequately? Undoubtedly some people have a gift for working with children. Others find it more difficult but are very committed and put a great deal of time and energy into their work. It is probably people in this category who benefit most from appropriate training, for the interest and motivation are there and it is possible to improve and develop skills. There are people who have no aptitude for pastoral work and do not find it easy to communicate freely with children except within, say, the formal context of a classroom. If their job demands a pastoral input, then it is essential that they are given sufficient training and back-up to help them achieve some degree of confidence in their dealings with children, for otherwise the criticisms which probably come their way are at the least unfair.

Qualities of good care staff

Qualities which are essential to the development of good pastoral skills are keeping an open mind, being willing to contemplate changing our attitudes and behaviour, and being prepared to look inside ourselves with a view to increasing our self-awareness. People who have close dealings with children cannot afford to forget that their own personalities have been forged by the same processes as those which are operating on the children in their charge. It is well known to psychotherapists that the inner lives of their clients can resonate with their own inner lives, sometimes so powerfully as to evoke responses which have little to do with the real person sitting in front of them. Our understanding of, and responses to, other people are always subject to our personal experiences and expectations, and working with children frequently brings back into play the anxieties, vulnerabilities and unfinished business of our own childhood. Being, or allowing ourselves to become, aware of the child who still lives in all of us can cause anxiety. Nevertheless it is essential if we are to perceive the children in our care with sufficient objectivity to be helpful in their emotional healing or development. Any person who is unwilling to turn the searchlight on himself when he is having difficulty in relating to a particular child or children, in order to examine his own contribution to the impasse, is unlikely to facilitate a successful outcome.

Gaining and improving pastoral skills

Pastoral staff do not need to become trained counsellors in order to be effective, and attitude is more important than aptitude when it comes to dealing with children. Genuine interest in them as individuals, coupled with respect for them as human beings, goes a very long way, and most children are very tolerant of personal idiosyncrasies if they know that the concern for them is real and consistent. (The converse is also true!) However, some basic counselling skills can increase the effectiveness of staff interventions a hundredfold, and some knowledge about how people develop enables carers to keep a realistic perspective and to make good judgements about the significance and seriousness of children's emotional or behavioural difficulties. For example, it is important to know when to refer a child to someone better equipped to deal with his particular problems.

Conclusion

Caring for children when they are separated from their families, whatever the reason for the separation, is a complex business. Residential work at all levels of responsibility is demanding at the best of times, but when it is attempted by people with little or no training, sometimes on top of a normal full-time job, sometimes by people who feel themselves to have low status within the organisation, then it is hard to believe that the care provided can consistently approach the 'good enough'. That it seems to do so in many instances is little short of miraculous. How much better could it be if everyone involved in it received the training they need and the recognition they deserve?

I have tried to provide a starting point for thinking about the kind of residential environment which will give children the best chance of optimal emotional and social development. If the environment is sufficiently supportive children will begin to reveal their problems and confusions, their dilemmas and their faulty and unhelpful beliefs about themselves and the world. Those who care for them need to be confident that they and the organisation can help the children deal safely and constructively with all that they bring to light. They will then have the immense satisfaction of knowing that those children at least who have been lucky enough to pass through their hands have been given the best possible preparation for adulthood. There are few jobs which offer that kind of reward.

CHAPTER 5

The Built Environment

Christopher King

Image and component parts

Boarding-school life is characterised and caricatured by the paradoxical images of its environment, fostered by the media and fed by literature. Elitism in the setting of the spartan atmosphere of a Dickensian workhouse perhaps best summarises that image. A 'concerned environment' within which the individual can develop is not something the latter day Oliver Twists are envisaged as enjoying. The picture of teachers with a superior air, dressed in gowns and wielding their discipline with an iron fist as boys sit in rows, chanting Latin verses and looking forward to cold showers and muscular games sessions is still accepted as the norm by many. However, those of us within the walls of such establishments, and here I am primarily concerned with the independent boarding school, know that the school of the early 1990s is a business.

In order to gain and retain the market, the independent school has responded by adjusting the package that it makes available to parents of potential pupils. That package has many facets, but significant amongst them are the setting and the physical environment. Robinson (1990) examined many of the relevant facets in drawing the distinction between the 'family' and the 'formal' paradigms. In the former the house parent aims for a close relationship with the pupil, and there is a

> drive to domesticate the boarding house and make it as much like home as possible, to compensate for the perceived deprivation (as result of the removal of daily emotional contact with parents and family) of the inmates. After the soft furnishings, kitchens and televisions, come smaller house groups of mixed ages.

In the latter, Robinson expresses the great virtue of boarding: boarding is different from family life and has certain advantages over it. Boarding should ideally complement the good family life, not simply supplement it, and the differences should be emphasised and extolled, not minimised and hidden under the new carpet. Boarding should provide a 'challenge', not from the regime but from 'those with whom the child eats, plays and sleeps'. The spartan, however, though lamented apparently in some quarters, in others appears to be on the way out, to be replaced by carpets, central heating and videos. Ambitious building programmes have been undertaken as no effort, or apparently expense, is spared to make sure that the physical manifestation of the package is up to date and reflects the current demands of the market.

Also significant within the package is the 'atmosphere' or 'social climate' within which the individual is guided towards the future. One instantly gains a 'feel' for any institution one enters. It is 'warm' or 'cold', is there a welcoming or distancing force evident? The educational process is played out on the school's environmental chessboard which is composed at one and the same time of the physical and social elements.

'Environment' is the buzz-word of the moment, but as such it is used far too glibly and deserves a far more detailed examination. It is important to remember that the environment exists at two levels; the objective and the perceived. The objective environment of residential schools has in turn two elements; the physical and the social climate. Moos (1974) says that human behaviour cannot be understood apart from the environmental context in which it occurs and that though there may be two elements to the environment, 'physical and social environments must be studied together'. This is, of course, entirely fair and many examples may be produced to illustrate the idea. Schools for instance that historically were built with close ties to monasteries or convents were often built in a similar style. This imposition of a monastic style extended to the enforcement of associated customs. For example earlier this century girls had to take baths in shifts and were not allowed to look at their own bodies when they were in the bath. If one is to gain a full appreciation of the total environment both elements should be viewed together but this chapter concentrates on the physical environment.

The physical environment is both natural and built. It has history and even though termed 'natural' invariably it is almost wholly managed. The physical environment supplies the ecological dimension with its attendant geographical, meteorological, architectural and design variables. The physical environment is listed as the primary determinant of behaviour by many researchers. Context, altitude, soil characteristics, humidity are some elements of the physical environment that have been specifically studied particularly. Phenomena of great importance have been attributed to the climate. In 1965 riots in Los Angeles and Chicago were widely believed to have, in part, had their origins in the particularly hot weather at that time. Similarly and more recently there would appear to be a significant correlation between the sustained period of hot, sultry weather during the summers of 1981 and 1985 and the rioting in several British inner city areas such as St Paul's in Bristol and Toxteth in Liverpool. Dramatically higher rates of suicide occur in times of depressional weather. School public examinations are almost invariably sat during the period of warmest, most humid meteorological conditions to the great discomfort of asthma and hay-fever sufferers.

To what extent the physical environment is the reinforcing 'stimulus' is perhaps something which can only be assessed in the context of individual events. More often it is thought that it is the 'setting event' which forms the conditions for the response to occur. Architects and designers often proceed on the assumption that there is a link between psychological events and environmental factors. Some colours are described as cheerful or gloomy. Red is often seen as a warm colour and blue as cold. The American architect, Frank Lloyd Wright, at times designed confining corridors in order that on entering an open space the contrast of openness and light would be enhanced. Slater and Lipman (1980) considered the effectiveness of design in creating an environment suitable for the care of the elderly. Although clearly the demands of old people are different in specifics from those of adolescents in a residential school, the principles suggested have a wider application. They suggested that the 'themes' for evaluation of the effectiveness of the environment should be: choice, independence, convenience, privacy and comprehensibility. It is interesting to note that the Children Act (1989) has taken up some of these themes in setting out the requirements for all residential schools.

In the context of choice, the boarding house of a residential school has a variety of functions imposed on it by the curriculum and extra-curricular activities offered by the school. Independence is a term to express the physical ability of the individual to move about the house. Corridor width and staircase position would be important here. Furniture and fittings may restrict or promote independence. Convenience often is arranged from the viewpoint of authority and the opportunity for pupils to affect the convenience of their house may be limited. However, convenience is a high priority for pupils. It is clear that there is a general desire to be in close proximity to particular school facilities such as the dining room, sports hall and classrooms. Privacy is underplayed traditionally in residential education and locks and keys are not generally available to pupils. Privacy or rather the lack of it may have a great effect on some pupils who may not be able to adjust to boarding life and the Children Act specifically requires this to be recognised. Privacy is important as a simple example illustrates. A girl of ten or eleven may still be thought of as a 'little girl' who is unconcerned at the prospect of standing naked in the shower. However, adolescence suddenly arrives and that same girl becomes prudish and hides her nakedness discreetly, if that is possible, behind the shower curtain. Comprehensibility concerns the ideas of familiarity and has many complex manifestations. A very important expression is the personalising by pupils of their rooms. Posters and magazine cuttings mixed with photographs and slogans reflect the personalities of individuals. An interpretation of such decorations is beyond the scope of this work. However there is no doubting the fact that the decoration or personalising of their rooms reflects the personality of the individual often set in the fashion of the time, but with a tempering element as a result of the ethos of the school.

   The built environment of the boarding school deserves particular attention. Frank Lloyd Wright, once defined design as 'art with a purpose'. If that is true then if we know the purpose behind a building in a residential school then we are well on our way to understand this particular built environment. The architect E.R. Robson (1972) said

> a school should appear like a school and not like a monastery, a town hall or a set of almshouses. Large towers and prodigious roofs, exaggerated gables ... are all better avoided.

By implication then this has not always been the case. The Clarendon Commission (1864) said of the collegiate architecture so evident in many of the public schools in existence in the 19th century that 'its development with emphasis on quadrangles, cloisters, and late Gothic styles may be seen as an attempt to emphasise the close links between public school and university'. Undoubtedly the association was made, and intentionally so, and the impact can be revealed in other ways even in the latter part of the 20th century.

A conversation overheard between two boys of a visiting school to Cheltenham College on the occasion of a cricket match:

'What chance have we got today?'
'Not much; have you seen the size of their chapel?'

The talent or otherwise of the home side was not assessed by the playing record or first-hand experience of their skill but by the imposing, 'superior' nature of the built environment. As the visiting member of staff said, his team had 'lost before the first ball was bowled'.

In recent years behavioural studies have highlighted the growing belief that the designed environment though it may not determine experience does at least support satisfaction, happiness and effectiveness in combination with social influences. The designed environment often, however, does not 'work' with respect to its impact on human experience. It can be awkward, even destructive rather than supportive of personal competence and growth. The temporal element should not be overlooked. What may have fitted the particular time when a building was conceived may not be so suitable a year, a decade or a century later.

Many of our residential schools retain buildings which were not built originally as schools. Even if they were, they belong to a different generation of thought on what makes good educational practice. They have been, in some but not all cases, modified, modernised and adapted but are they always suited to their use? Debate on such issues is not new of course; throughout the second half of the 19th century the debate was for and against the teaching by 'divisions'. That is, that much teaching took place in one large, imposing room but with the pupils subdivided into 'divisions' where different members of staff would conduct different lessons. Physical distinction of those 'divisions' was rare but as the century progressed so developed the argument for single classrooms. Eton up to 1885 had 'up to three divisions' taught regularly in one room, but as a result of an energetic building programme, by 1886 each group was taught in a single classroom. There is little evidence of peoples' perceptual view of classrooms at that time. However in an argument advanced by the President of the Royal Institute of British Architects (RIBA) at the end of the century he claimed that 'the aesthetic crudity of many English industrial products could be attributed to the influence of ugly classrooms' (Robson, 1972). Thus there is a need for a more relevant appraisal of the residential environment. It is curious and a paradox that often the most impressive building externally is a considerable disappointment on the inside. Many a prestigious school possesses the most impressive façade but internally appears cold, dark and uninviting. In contrast the often bland functional external look of the unacclaimed school can conceal a warmth, lightness and a degree of comfort that delights.

In the latter part of the 20th century the urge to build has been a major motivating force. In many cases the buildings constructed by schools have had their origins in the desire to present a dynamic modern outlook, with a wave of language laboratories, computer suites, and technology departments being built as new educational fashions emerged. Piecemeal modernisation is another characteristic of the last 25 years as many schools have had to wrestle with the fact that they have ancient and listed buildings dictating the style, at least externally, that their schools must adopt.

Factors that shape the built environment

The built environment is just part of the physical environment with its history and visible character. However, its fuller personality is determined by the complex interplay of other factors that exert an influence on the decision makers who create the managed physical environment.

The other environmental characteristic is the social climate. Moos (1974) says that 'the character of an environment is dependent in part of the typical characteristics of its members', and again that, 'the college environment depends on the personal characteristics of the students, faculty, administration and staff of the institution'. The logical conclusion from this is that different schools have different climates determined by the stated goals of the school and the pupils' practical interpretation resulting from their perception of those goals.

Schools, including residential ones, which are often in remote rural areas may by physically cut off from the outside world but still do not exist in isolation. They are conditioned by factors external and internal to society and it may be that they are unable wholly to direct their own destinies. Government action, the prevailing financial climate and competition amongst similar schools are bound to shape thoughts and attitudes within them. Other factors which must bear powerfully on their aims, means and effectiveness are those of history and tradition, together with the culture of their staffs, parents and pupils.

There is danger at this point that the discussion can drift into a listing of innumerable factors that affect residential schools since these might be merely the factors that affect society in general. A summary diagram (Figure 2) identifies the major forces responsible for shaping the social environment.

By showing the physical and social climatic boundary as an ellipse that is closed, the implication is that the institution is 'closed'. Lambert (1975) made the following observation:

> though all schools belong to the species of organisations, boarding schools differ from day schools in that they are closed or 'total' societies. Such societies are marked by the exercise of complete control over their members' behaviour and value orientations by the provision of all their basic necessities within their boundaries.

He did go on to point out that residential schools are in some senses only partially 'total' in that, 'their members leave at the end of every term and then are exposed to the freedoms and the values of the wider society' and 'other outsiders may be admitted from time to time'. These comments were published in 1975 but reflected the situation as it was in the late 1960s and early 1970s. They could not reflect the critical period between 1974 and 1976 when the full effects of inflation, particularly in relation to teachers' pay awards as a result of the Houghton Review, saw increases in fees of 35.29 per cent for small HMC boarding schools and 32.91 per cent for major HMC boarding schools, all set against a rate of inflation of 26 per cent during the year September 1974 to September 1975. These figures from Rae (1981) were for the 'critical' years. As a result, the parents looked for, even demanded, and achieved, more influence on the schools' activities. Even more significant was the way in which schools increasingly recognised that they

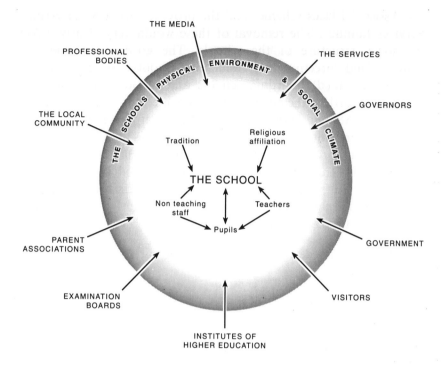

Figure 2   Social Environment

were businesses, competing in the market place. This is reflected in the model of forces affecting the social climatic environment of the residential school. Inside the boundary are the elements of the closed system although this does not necessarily mean stagnation. A series of internal loops is identified which represent stability and the known social atmosphere. However the residential school is very obviously affected by a number of external influences that shape the alumni and image.

Government influence on the built environment

The government has an enormous influence on residential schools both at a local and a national level. The scale of this influence affects many facets of life ranging from fire regulations to corporal punishment. One of the more significant ways in which it affects residential bodies is through their charitable status of such schools, the Assisted Places scheme, and the provision of fees for Armed Services families. The removal of these would very clearly affect the social structure of the schools. The government does, of course, fund directly some residential schools, for example the state (maintained) boarding schools and schools with specialist functions. Further, the government has made wide-ranging changes to GCSE, AS and modified A levels. What the impact of the National Curriculum will have, we shall have, is as yet conjectural. All represent forces acting upon the boarding environment.

Specifically the built environment is regulated by two precise instruments. Firstly, the Children Act (1989) sets the context for other specific requirements of governmental legislation. It says in the introductory statements:

> When a court determines any question with respect to:
>
> (a) the upbringing of a child; or
> (b) the administration of a child's property or the application of any income arising from it,
>
> the child's welfare shall be the court's paramount consideration.

The key word here is 'welfare' as throughout the Act it is this that individuals and institutions are charged to guarantee. The Act contains many specific mechanisms intended to direct such people and organisations to achieve this aim and in part XII, it says 'where a child is provided with accommodation by any health authority or local education authority ("the accommodation authority")' the local authority ('the responsible authority'), shall be notified and 'take such steps as are reasonably practicable to enable them to determine whether the child's welfare is adequately safeguarded and promoted while he is accommodated by the accommodating authority.'

In a similar fashion the legislation extends to include children accommodated in independent schools where

> it shall be the duty of –
>
> (a) the proprietor of any independent school which provides accommodation for any child; and
> (b) any person who is not the proprietor of such a school but is responsible for conducting it,
>
> to safeguard and promote the child's welfare.

The Act goes on to make the local authority responsible for determining whether the 'child's welfare is adequately safeguarded and promoted while he is accommodated by the school'. In effect, the local authority has to develop a system of inspections and a procedure to be followed in order to satisfy themselves as Social Service Authorities that the welfare of the child is achieved.

What is not clear is what will be expected as 'necessary to safeguard the welfare of the child' in terms of the dimensions, proportions and aesthetics of the built environment in boarding schools. For ideas we can turn to the second Government Instrument, The Education (School Premises) Regulations 1981, no. 909, which applies to boarding schools in the maintained sector. A maintained boarding school is defined in the Statutory Instrument as 'a school with boarding pupils whether or not it has day pupils'. This Instrument is currently under review at the Department of Education and Science and the possibility is that the future Instrument will be somewhat less precise in its prescription. However, the existing Instrument is likely, in at least the immediate future, to be the best guide to good practice. Part IV specifically relates to the boarding accommodation and includes the following detailed requirements.

The school 'shall include sleeping accommodation for the number of boarding pupils thereat' and where pupils have attained the age of eight 'the sleeping accommodation shall be such that such boys and girls are not required to share a dormitory'.

A dormitory

shall be such that –

(a) the floor area is not less than the aggregate of $4.2m^2$ for each pupil sleeping therein and $1.6m^2$, and
(b) there is a distance of not less than 900mm between any two beds. A cubicle for a pupil shall have its own window and shall be of a floor area not less than $5.0m^2$.
A bedroom for a pupil shall be of a floor area not less than $6.0m^2$.

The washroom accommodation is detailed with the requirement that it should be distributed throughout the building so as to be reasonably accessible to the sleeping accommodation and that specifically:

there shall be at least one water closet for every 5 boarding pupils.

There shall be at least one washbasin –

(a) for every 3 of the first 60 boarding pupils;
(b) for every 4 of the next 40 boarding pupils, and
(c) for every further 5 boarding pupils.

There shall be at least one bath or shower for every 10 pupils and at least a quarter of the minimum number of such fittings shall be baths.

The 'living accommodation' meaning the area used for the purposes of private study and for social purposes should be at the rate of 2.3m² per pupil but reduced where such things as study bedrooms are employed. All these points are very specific and a host of other requirements are made of the school as a whole. These include the provision of sick rooms, dining and food preparation areas, and even an airing room, sewing room and storage space for bedding. A number of structural requirements are made but in general terms. Such things as fire prevention, heating, lighting, acoustics and water provision are broadly covered by measures clearly intended to ensure the welfare of the child. For example,

Washbasins, baths, showers, water closets and urinals shall have an adequate supply of cold water and washbasins, baths and showers shall also provide an adequate supply of warm water, in the case of baths and showers, at a temperature not exceeding 43.5 degrees C.

It would seem that the inspections by local authorities must involve the use of tape measure, thermometer and calculator!

There are clearly some problems with such instructions as certain issues are not acknowledged. For instance, in the case of the dimensions for dormitory or bedroom the steep incline of a sloping ceiling may severely inhibit the movement and comfort of an individual. The question of the ratio of urinals to WCs is another 'grey' area. A finer point of debate is the matter of differing types of requirement according to custom of use. For example, does the size and quality of room, furniture and fittings have to be the same for a pupil who is in residence for only four nights per week compared to a pupil who is in the house on a permanent basis?

The final and perhaps most useful clues as to what might be expected of the built environment come from the HMI report *Boarding in Maintained Schools: A Survey* (1990).

This report was written following the inspection of boarding provision in 43 Local Education Authority maintained schools in England during the period January 1986 to March 1990. In the course of visiting, HMI developed and refined in the light of experience, criteria for what constitutes good physical provision and features of good practice. They made many observations which give direction to thoughts on what the built environment should contain. They said:

1) In the houses that were seen to be in very good decorative order it was clear that the boarders took very great care of their environment and were proud of their surroundings.

2) For most youngsters who board, dormitories and bedrooms are reasonably comfortable and most have carpeted floors which add to the feeling of homeliness and privacy.... Although furnishing is generally satisfactory, storage space for boarders' clothes and other belongings is often limited.

They cite examples of shared cupboards, wardrobes and situations where boarders, 'were unable to create any sense of presence let alone ownership of their rooms'. There is concern that a deep sense of rootlessness could be acquired by boarders in this situation. However, they went on to state that instances of very poor practice are rare and

it is heartening to see how increasingly schools are looking to purpose-designed furniture of good robust quality, pleasant to the eye and in keeping with the needs of the boarders concerned.

3) In all schools visited there were sufficient numbers of wash basins, baths and showers and toilets as defined by Statutory Instrument 909. It is of course important that these are well maintained to ensure privacy is retained.

4) It is considered important that the provision of common rooms, television rooms and indoor games should be as broad and unrestricted as practically possible. It was noted that 'too often ... it is very difficult for younger children to separate

themselves from older'. Where the house caters for boarders with mild behavioural or emotional difficulties the nature of the distribution of spaces for children to withdraw and let off steam is crucial. Does a house have rooms set aside for hobbies, games and quiet for individuals and small groups? The report goes on to say 'when considering developing common space schools should always consider these alternative possibilities as very proper means to extend the quality and variety of spaces available for boarders'.

5) In too many cases the boarders' library 'is confined to a shelf in a corridor or a small cupboard in a public room and stocked with out of date and often tatty story and reference books'. Poor provision of newspapers and journals was also noted. A library of quality and the taking of periodicals and newspapers are thought to be good practice.

6) Many boarding houses have little in the way of public space. Nevertheless what there is can be important in helping to create an overall ethos which visitors can appreciate on entering.

7) On the subject of personal space and privacy the HMI commented almost all schools allow boarders to personalise the space around their beds with posters and pictures although in many instances there is insufficient pin-board space to allow this to be done neatly and attractively. 'The creation of such semi-private space for boarders is of great importance in their social development.'

8) It was commented that girls' rooms were often arranged so as to produce 'a homely atmosphere' but also that

much boys' accommodation [is] also attractively arranged and personalised with the sensitive use of plants. This most often occurs where boarding staff actively encourage boys to be conscious of the quality of their personal and shared environments.

9) The comment on housekeeping forms a neat summary of the forces that determine the state of the environment within the house.

There are two contradictory elements in managing a house which need a measure of reconciliation. The first is the need to maintain a tidy and hygienic environment and the second is the need to create a homely atmosphere in which the boarders can live comfortably. Most houses are well managed without destroying a necessary degree of cosy untidiness.

In Appendix A of the HMI Report the Inspectors state what they regard as 'good boarding provision'. This 'consists of a complex and successful interplay of often very subtle factors'. Given that, the first elements for good boarding provision should include:

Accommodation that is of a reasonable standard in its state of maintenance and decoration. Particular considerations will be given by the school to health and safety matters and to setting good aesthetic standards.

The report continues:

The availability of a wide range of kinds of space for boarders to live in. Boarders will have personal and semi-private space, space to carry out a range of activities and space to get away from it all. Boarding staff will be aware of the importance of space both in the buildings and outside, including grounds, and of the importance of access to local facilities. Boarders inhabit a closely communal world which ranges from the personal, small and private through open, populous and at times noisy and boisterous and the characteristics of both accommodation and organisation will reflect this.

Here then are a multitude of clues as to what should be inspected and questioned in any survey of good boarding provision for the welfare of the children. But things are not as simple as just listing all items that go to make up a good boarding environment. In the Department of Health *The Welfare of Children in Boarding Schools: Practice Guide* (1991) general but significant comments are made concerning the common rooms, bedrooms, dining rooms and sanitary accommodation. This guide was written to assist Social Services Departments in implementing their duty to inspect independent boarding schools. It says that

Common room space should be sufficient for the age and number of boarders present in a house. It is important to have a range of rooms (in the house or close by and accessible in the school) for boarders to relax and follow a variety of indoor activities.

The opportunity should exist for the boarder to pursue quiet as well as the more boisterous activities. 'Furniture and accommodation should be in a good decorative order.' 'All pupils should have access to snack and hot-drink making facilities.' In respect of bedrooms they should be 'warm and comfortable and not overcrowded. Beds should always have space to store personal possessions in their own lockable cupboards . . . and space that they can personalise'. There should be telephone facilities available for boarders.

Oxfordshire Social Services Department (SSD) was one of the four authorities to carry out pilot investigations with a view to implementing the Children Act (1989). Oxfordshire decided that when it came to the built environment it was important to have some form of base line and for that they took Instrument 909. They found that one of the key issues that had to be addressed occurred under Section 63 of the Act. This section refers to children's homes but it says that 'an independent school is a children's home if it provides accommodation for not more than fifty children'. The attitude of the SSD is critical here for in Volume 4 of the Guidance and Regulations relating to the Act there are far more statements on the principles to be followed in the establishment of the built environment of a children's home. The decision on this determines which standards are to be applied to pupils who are regarded as being at a school.

The work of Morgan with the Oxfordshire Social Services has led to a Department of Health (1992) publication on the views of pupils on boarding. A few of the most frequently and strongly held views according to Morgan are that the preferred dormitory size is for four or five pupils. However, the older age range at any level in a school, be it preparatory or 13–18 secondary school age, have a preference for single studies. The one most consistent criticism of boarding houses cited by pupils was of noise invading their privacy. On the question of washing facilities, individual showers were considered to be the best. Privacy was not found to be an issue but there is a move away from communal washing though it is more acceptable following games or sporting activities. Plumbing is considered an important subject by the SSDs, particularly the provision of hot water and the control of its temperature. According to Morgan, a major criticism of boarders is the unreliability of hot water supply and the variability of its temperature. For the SSD there is the concern for the disabled or individuals who are because of age or disability unable to discriminate water temperature, being injured by water that is too hot. Related to this is the question of the temperature of surfaces such as radiators. In this area the school and the SSD will have to negotiate when dealing with physically able young people.

When one comes to consider and then assess the merits or otherwise of the school environment the individual receives a plethora of stimuli, the product of all the forces previously discussed. Nevertheless, the impact made upon that individual results from an overview of the total school created by the sum of the individual stimuli.

It would seem plausible that two or more individuals of disparate backgrounds meeting to discuss the environment of a residential school could be expected to agree in large measure on their assessment of the built environment. Many of the above points can be noted and recorded on a simple tick list. The answer to the question; is that building made of brick? is simple. However, the answer to the question; of what kind of brick is that building constructed? may bring a far wider range of answers. A brick can be London, red or blue, but it can also be cold, bare or majestic. The environment, it seems, is in the eye of the beholder and open to an individual's perception of it.

How individuals perceive the world in which they live is something about which the residential school is much exercised at the present time as it undertakes the task of projecting an attractive image. The Independent Schools' Information Service (ISIS) provides a forum for the independent schools to project their image and recently the state boarding schools have formed their own organisation to perform much the same task.

Under the heading 'The Lure of the Blackboard Jungle' in the *Daily Telegraph*, Rachel Billington (1991) writes on her observations of how parents select a school for their offspring:

> Oh for the luxury and the agony of choosing schools! The shiny prospectuses appear, like travel brochures, depicting stately homes chock-a-bloc with computer labs and Olympic sized swimming pools. Outside, the rugger fields writhe with eager boys who play under great oaks planted by Capability Brown.

The image of the best of the old combined with the best of the new sells itself to the parents who gain the added advantage of seeing the tangible evidence that they need to justify to themselves the substantial financial outlay. This superficiality is not enough for the more discerning to assess the effectiveness of a school and there follows an attempt to supply a more exacting assessment of the built environment.

Evaluation of the designed environment

In an ideal situation those responsible for commissioning, designing and building residential schools would be able to predict the environmental consequences of proposed developments. If the purpose is known then ideally one should design in the knowledge of the impact that design will have. Prediction of that impact can only follow from a substantive empirical base and as yet there is no such base. In order to progress, therefore, evaluation is the first stage. If we could predict how well buildings are 'known' those responsible for promoting, designing and modifying them would have a powerful design tool. To do this it is necessary to assess perceptions of the built environment and discover those elements that capture attention and hold a place in the inhabitant's mental representation of his residential environment.

Appleyard (1969) discussed these issues in relation to the planning of the new city of Cuidad Guayana, Venezuela. Three hundred interviews were carried out relating to the inhabitants' perceptions of the city. They set out to discover how the people viewed the city. Was it seen in terms of its land uses, as physical forms and spaces or did they see it as an economic or political structure? Did they picture the city as a social pattern, a kind of mental layout of the census data or as a setting for personal activities, or was it to them a sensuous environment of sights, sounds, colours and textures?

His evidence suggests that unless a building is seen it cannot project an image. Visibility is a necessary component for recall. If a building is distinct in form it may be little known except amongst those who use it regularly. A building's importance can be measured by three attributes:

(1) its viewpoint intensity: and estimate of the number of people who might regularly see it;
(2) its viewpoint significance: its position at important decision points of transition for pedestrians or traffic; and
(3) its immediacy: a measure of its distance from obvious viewpoints.

The final point emerged as significant when it was realised that physically and functionally insignificant buildings at major decision points such as entrances were frequently recalled.

The attributes of the physical form that most influenced recall seemed to be movement, contour, size, shape and surface. Movement of people seems to be the main factor, with such things as recreation areas or areas where queues occur being noted. Contour, the relative surface expression of the building concerning such things as the sharpness of a building's boundary from its surroundings, is especially important with individual buildings. Size of a building was of only moderate importance as was shape, though this factor took on a greater significance when buildings possessed a complexity that gave uniqueness.

Surface colour, though noted, was of slight significance because it seems that buildings in any one area tend to be of similar colour. Signs and notices also, and perhaps surprisingly, have little impact. Important buildings often have only modest signs, and places of importance to the individual are only rarely identified from signs. Such perceptual work gives strong clues as to how people without any formal evaluation procedure may view the built environment in which they live and work. However, to rely on recall for effective assessment of the built environment would only provide a very selective picture of the total environment.

Evaluation should involve consideration of at least four factors according to Friedman *et al.* (1978), and their ideas concerning what should be evaluated in the social and historical context are illustrated in the summary diagram (Figure 3).

The setting

The physical environment in which people operate is crucial to evaluation. The physical environment must be after all what the designer works with and produces. The setting where relevant would include the following:

1) Organisational goals and needs such as: which factors such as satisfaction, results, finance are most highly valued and by whom?

2) Organisational functioning such as: which groups affect others? Which groups need to communicate? Which groups have priority in affecting the goals and values mentioned above? House staff one would expect to have close, even immediate contact with the pupils in their charge but what about the headmaster with his 'office', and Common Room?

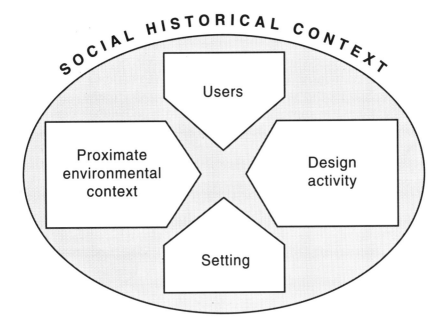

Figure 3

Are the founders' principles followed today as at the establishment of the school? Do parents or generous benefactors
have considerable influence on school policy?

3) Fabric and design: the setting may determine the materials
used, for example 'Cotswold' stone in Gloucestershire.

4) Ambient qualities such as noise, light and temperature: these
are elements which may also have symbolic value.

5) Symbols: these would include study size and position which
may vary according to authority in the boarding house.

6) Condition of the setting, such as the quality of the maintenance or changes and decorations provided by the users: it
may be formal in the sense of paint colours and the state of
plaster on the walls. It can be informal in the sense of posters,
cards and graffiti added by pupils.

The users

The ultimate test of the success of a design setting is its ability to
support explicit and implicit human needs and values. A typical list

of users might include, besides the house staff and children, the governors, the headteacher, the teaching staff, the administrative staff, the parents, the maintenance staff and neighbours who are affected by the building. Research methods that observe behaviour without affecting it may not always be possible or morally justifiable, but some knowledge of user perspectives, preferences, needs and values is essential. Their group activity patterns are largely determined by the school routine but also by individual characteristics such as age, sex, income and home background.

The proximate environmental context

Each setting exists in a neighbourhood and is affected by such factors as: climate, air quality, water quality, transportation, cultural/social facilities and safety.

The design process

It has been stated by professionals that design is the weakest area of the whole evaluation process. The personalities involved in the design process bring to it their own values, preferences and attitudes, whilst in addition there are numerous directives, limitations and criteria. These include directives of the Department of Education and Science as well as Acts of Parliament which may cover everything from building practice to curriculum content. Local government and in particular the planning authorities with related bodies and their officers such as the Fire Prevention Officer exert a form of design evaluation which is intended to produce a more effective environment. Clearly politically related influences may be susceptible to sudden dramatic fluctuations in direction and emphasis.

Financial constraints also have an obvious influence on any project. This truism has perhaps had the biggest single influence on residential school building design.

Socio-historical context

A common situation encountered by many residential schools is that a project judged as a success on its completion is seen differently at a later date. Social and political trends affect the building, and evaluation schemes if they are to be of value must be applicable to buildings of considerable age. Of course in time all buildings do need replacement but what is the cycle of replacement? Newness in no way guarantees the creation of excellence.

Towards design evaluation

Several workers have undertaken research in areas closely related to training and in particular the University Residence Environment Scale (URES) as developed by Moos of Stamford University and Gerst of the University of California (Moos, 1974 and 1975) is useful. This method of evaluating the environment grew out of a recognition by Moos that there are both environmental and personal systems. Most environments admit new members selectively. Certainly there is an element in selection to most residential schools. People may also select the environment they wish to enter and senior pupils may either positively select a new school or, by inertia, make the choice to stay put when a change might be available. Moos said that the environmental and personal systems affect each other through 'mediating' processes. The pupil, on entering an environment, will adapt to it using a set of 'coping' skills but at the same time he may have the effect of changing the system stability or change may be the outcome. In Moos' own example he cites the college setting orientated towards traditional religious values and academic accomplishment which may help students to maintain their religious beliefs and to increase their aspirations and achievement levels.

Moos claims that there is an infinite number of environmental variables but they can be conceptualised into four major domains: the physical setting; organisational factors; the human aggregate; and the social climate. Each of these domains can influence educational outcomes directly or indirectly. Moos was most concerned with how the social climate is determined by and mediates the influence of the other three domains. Together with Gerst, Moos set out to develop a way to measure the social environments of student living groups and to obtain information about the usual pattern of behaviour that occurs within them. They were interested in considering the perceptions of the living group as it was by that means only that they could discover the 'reality' of that setting. As a result they developed the URES to measure the social environments of campus living groups, such as dormitories, fraternities and sororities. They identified three basic forms of the URES:

(1)   a 100 item Form R (real form) to assess the actual living unit;

(2)   an ideal living unit; and

(3)   a 100 item Form E (expectations form) to assess incoming students' or staff members expectations of a living group.

The underlying concept is that the objective consensus of individuals characterises their environment by defining the social or normative climate which exerts an influence on students' attitudes and behaviours.

In concluding his work Moos remarked that people are not 'passively moulded' by their environments but that neither are their environments passively moulded by them. Pupils at residential schools may however have only limited power to select or change their environments.

Using the principles established from the discussion and in the spirit of the Children Act (1989), an attempt has been made to design a scheme for the evaluation of the design environment. It might be argued that the questionnaire (Appendix 2) could be more rigorous but it is not intended to be definitive. Through its flexibility it may be adapted to particular situations. The use of the 'comment' column is intended to allow elaboration beyond the simple scoring system. It is suggested that for full value to be gained from such an evaluation, all users including the pupils should act as respondents.

CHAPTER 6

The Problem Decelerating Environment Approach: Putting the 1989 Children Act into Action

Alan J. Davison

The Problem Decelerating Environment Approach has been developed as a means of managing the emotional, psychological and physical elements of residential environments so that children, accommodated away from home, are offered the opportunity to achieve a level of personal development commensurate with their individual needs and circumstances. Although the Approach has generally been developed within the context of the care and education of disturbed and disruptive adolescents, and has been linked to long-term research and development programmes, application of the concepts inherent in the Problem Decelerating Environment are not restricted to residential child care and boarding-school settings. The Problem Decelerating Environment Approach has relevance to all situations in which people relate to each other, be it adult to child, manager to staff, or professional to client. The Approach is here described within virtual closed institution terms, forming a direct link with the philosophy inherent in the 1989 Children Act and its accompanying documentation. The philosophy of the Problem Decelerating Environment is based upon concepts explaining the psychological processes involved in child development, particularly those involving perception and the development of mental or internal models, the development of individual orientation and the dual nature of self (Davison, 1989). These concepts are seen as the basis for the application of a number of important processes including 'claiming', 'enabling', and 'democratisation'. An attempt will be made to explain elements of these processes but it must be stressed that the Problem

Decelerating Environment Approach can only be offered in an outline form within the context of this text.

The psychological basis of the Problem Decelerating Environment Approach

Establishing integrity

The basic premiss of the Problem Decelerating Environment is that there is no circumstance under which a child can be viewed as a possession. Children are a responsibility and a commitment for those adults who are charged with their care, control and development. There is an inherent acceptance that each child has a fundamental, individual integrity which consists of the right to be oneself. This is based upon an understanding that the core of all human interaction lies in the perceptual events which occur between individuals, and not upon a blind faith in the power of hierarchical structures. Children are people. Individual people are unique and they have the right to expect that their uniqueness will be respected in their dealings with others. Children should expect no less. The 1989 Children Act attempts to dispense with the vast amount of piecemeal and highly confusing legislation previously directed at protecting and controlling children. In its place it creates a means of ensuring that the law and society put the child's needs and welfare first in all cases, emphasising parental responsibility and directing that parents and professionals should form partnerships which will ensure that the child's welfare is always the primary consideration.

The Paramountcy Principle, enshrined within the 1989 Children Act, emphasises the centrality of children's needs and the need to take into account the child's wishes in all decisions affecting that child. It first appears in section 1.1 (a) and (b) of the Act and is variously repeated throughout the Children Act literature (see Volume 4., paragraph, 1.1.; Volume 5., paragraph 2.4.1). If the challenge is to be taken up within residential and boarding environments it is essential that staff are able to,

a) understand the nature of each individual child's feelings, needs, expectations, beliefs, hopes and aspirations;

b) to understand what happens when children are brought together into group living and educational environments;

c) to base such understandings on an awareness of culture, gender, and social and religious issues.

Understanding the world

The basis of residential group care and education is the inter-action between individual people who have during their lifetimes, constructed their own individual internal models of the external world in which they live. The internal model is shaped from the various aspects of the person's own unique experiences of the world, encompassing their total life environments. It is a personal reference source by which the individual can understand what it is that is being encountered in the external world. As the individual encounters things in the world, representations of those things, their properties and connections, along with the emotions they have generated and many other elements, are stored within the growing internal mental model. This initial 'seeing something as something' is an act of cognition. When the individual encounters these things again, reference is made to the internal model, a match is made and the individual is able to recognise these things, thus giving sense and meaning to both events in the world and the behaviour of others. This is the act of re-cognition.

The understanding gained from comparing the events seen in the world with the events stored in memory provides the basis for the individual's own response patterns. As each person experiences things in different ways, at different times, in different contexts and from different levels of involvement, the internal models which are formed are not only unique, they are also highly arbitrary constructions. In this way, each person's way of understanding the world is dependent upon the processes of perception applied by that individual. As such processes are largely arbitrary, the way in which something is understood is largely dependent upon how it was understood when it was first seen, and partly by the subsequent modifications made during further experiences of it. If one person sees something in a different way to the way in which it is seen by someone else, there is the basis of disagreement. If it is seen in the same way, there will be agreement. The way in which individuals see things is the basis of all the certainties and beliefs upon which they depend in their interactions with others and involvement with events in the external world.

Social groupings depend upon a high degree of perceptual consistency in order to maintain group cohesion and social conformity. In the group care setting, as in all areas of human interaction, it is important to understand what is meant when the phrases, 'I know', 'I believe', 'It's true' and 'I am certain', are uttered. An inability to understand the way in which a person's past experience builds up a unique and individual model of the world, and the extent to which that model governs the person's behaviour, can lead to situations of conflict in which one individual strives to change the other person's view of reality by imposing a perception of reality that is uniquely his own (Flekoy, 1991: 107). Individuals have the right to develop as unique and separate individuals, attaining an internal model balance between mutually or socially cohesive structures, and personal and individual structures.

Sharing the world

When people live together in groups, it is important that the way in which they see the world has a core of understanding which they can hold in common. Members of the group should have the facility to develop a series of communally accepted understandings which they can share and promulgate through communal involvement and the sharing of life experiences, but they must also have access to individual opportunities by which they can maintain their individuality within the group. An institution which places children in groups and provides only one set of experiences for all the children in the group, destroys individuality and creates institutionalised children. The Problem Decelerating Environment Approach operates from the basis that each child is unique and that spark of individuality must be maintained, supported and protected. This is not to argue that the child should not be directed in developmental tasks by adults. Each child is a member of a number of social groups, all of which depend upon the establishment and maintenance of shared understandings and expectations, subject to laws, rules and regulations. The difficulty facing those who work with children is to maintain a balance between maintaining the child's individuality and promoting the child's ability to attain appropriate social group membership.

The quality of the human environment creates the personal and social conditions by which individuals achieve their actualisation, becoming the person that they are capable of being (Maslow, 1943). Appropriate institutional quality control demands that managers focus upon the needs of the individual child as being of paramount importance, regardless of the number of children for whom the establishment provides care. The child as an individual must take precedence to the group as a unit.

High academic achievements, great sporting prowess and distinguished artistic endeavours can only achieve value if they are produced by a child who is also able to make other appropriate and healthy emotional and psychological developments. The child must be enabled to cope appropriately with all areas of life. Individually focused caring and the enabling of individual residents does not compromise larger establishments, or prevent them from meeting the individual needs of the large groups of children for whom they provide care and education, but it does stress the need to ensure that the environment is pro-active and professionally controlled rather than reactive and unplanned. It also raises important questions about the ratio of caring adults to children in the living environment. The philosophy of the establishment must be child centred and it must pervade all corners of the establishment and underpin the actions of every member of the community. It requires a realistic and humanitarian view of the child's place in the system and an agreed enabling view of the way in which the environment should be structured.

Individual orientation

It is essential that those who control the human environment understand the way in which the residents and staff respond to the environment in which they live. Within any establishment there will always be a range of individual responses to institutional structures and daily events, and whilst this places pressure upon the system, it also serves to enrich the quality of life in the living environment. Individuality should not be a problem although individuals sharing the same living arena can prove problematic. It is the mechanism of perceiving and reacting which must be understood if the establishment is to avoid abusing children by default, naively expecting that they will all cope and respond in the same way, for the same reasons. Each person's development is unique. They learn how to deal with the world in a manner which most suits their own personality as developed in specific settings with specific primary others acting as models. Each person has his or her own individual orientation with the world and that orientation is inherent in their own identity and personality.

Some children may deal with the world directly through *action-oriented behaviour*, instinctively and somewhat impulsively. They enjoy physical involvement and tend to tackle problems and challenges through action, the process of 'doing'. Other children may operate through the manipulation of their own internal model of the world via *introspection-oriented behaviour*, the process of 'thinking'. The latter group of children continually make reference to their own internal model of the world in order to understand what it is that is happening in the external world. They are able to understand what is happening because they are able to 'think out' what is happening. The truth of any situation is confirmed internally and then applied externally. Action-oriented children may make relatively few references to their internal model, preferring to act out into the world in a spontaneous and unthinking way. With time most children adopt a mixture of these two responses, sometimes 'thinking about', trying to make sense of the world, at others 'acting out', indulging in spontaneous reactions. A child who is too inclined to deal with the world through a dependence upon his internal model may appear withdrawn and out of touch with the world. There may be little actual involvement with the real world, attention being addressed entirely to 'working things out'. The child who is highly action oriented may appear to be unpredictable and uncontrolled, learning little from experience and often making the same mistakes over and over again.

In the residential care and boarding settings it is essential when working with children, and indeed with colleagues, to understand the other person's predisposition to one of these orientations. A child who is highly action oriented will not be too susceptible to verbal intervention through counselling or discussion sessions, and may feel intimidated and threatened by attempts by others to make him think out situations. A person who is highly introspective will not respond well to being plunged into a constant stream of physical activities and physical interactions. Attempts to enforce such involvement may create a great deal of upset and pain. Indeed members of staff should try to identify their own orientations and assess the effect it has upon the relationships they have with children. The folk-lore cameos in which the rugby master disparagingly taunts the intellectual child as 'weak' and 'effeminate', or, the academic teacher belittles the rugby playing child as 'thick' and 'insensitive' are not entirely figments of the imagination, but one must ask, which aspect of the human environment gives permission for such abuse to take place? Surely the official regime did not. The human environment has to enable an understanding of the difference between the two individual orientations and create enough space for both to live happily side by side.

When working with children who are action oriented it is useful to structure situations which will encourage introspection. Often such children have not been required to develop the ability to think clearly or to work things out in a logical and useful manner. Simple language structures and a dependency on non-linguistic communication skills may well be a sign of such an orientation. Although action-oriented behaviour may have proved satisfactory in meeting children's needs to date, as children mature, the world in which they find themselves makes increasing demands upon their introspective abilities. Similarly, highly introspective children may miss out on the wide range of social and personal cues which are available to them by not attending to the external world sufficiently. Children with little experience of action-oriented behaviour can easily become alienated within their peer group especially where the social currency consists largely of sporting prowess and physical expertise. If it is not possible to give constant attention to each child's adjustment and developmental needs then it is necessary to ensure that children are cared for in an environment which does not penalise their individuality, repress their natural orientation or abuse their vulnerability.

The Problem Decelerating Environment Approach: the key elements

The Problem Decelerating Environment Approach is a philosophy of care which provides a unifying philosophical basis and a practical orientation, enabling healthy individual growth and promoting openness. The main aim of the approach is to reduce negative stimuli and problem-accelerating elements within the environment in such a way as to best enable the full and healthy development of each child according to his or her own potential. Individual rights can only stand alongside individual responsibilities. There are a number of key elements in the Problem Decelerating Environment Approach which when established together create a philosophical basis within which the various developmental and institutional tasks can be framed. These key elements can be described in the following code of practice.

1) The child must be protected from unnecessary or inappropriate professional, community and family interventions.
2) The child must be protected from the range of institutional stressors, often seen as hassles, which relate to daily living requirements and institutional expectations.
3) Staff must promote feelings of security and safety as a basis for enabling the child to meet normal developmental tasks.
4) Staff must seek to enable the child to develop appropriate self-regarding sentiments.
5) Staff must enable the child to gain control over the direction of his or her own life.
6) Staff must strive to provide an environment in which there is mutual respect for individual integrity and the promotion of individual rights.
7) Staff must utilise an appropriate control of decision-making and risk-taking, including handling failure, in order to promote the individual child's physical, social, psychological and emotional development. Each must 'own' their own behaviour.
8) Staff must seek to establish an appropriate balance between the child's short-term and long-term needs, and between the demands of living in the residential environment and the world outside.
9) Staff must ensure that the physical environment reflects the level of esteem in which the child is held.
10) An appropriate monitoring of care provision must be ongoing.
11) Staff should offer a range of primary and secondary, physical and intellectual, personal and social opportunities for each child according to their individual orientation.
12) Staff must ensure that children have an appropriate link with their own history, being able to establish links with

their past and promote their own identity in the present and future.

Protecting the child

The child must be protected from unnecessary or inappropriate professional, community or family interventions. The child has individual needs which have to be addressed during development. Within the family, parents are charged with the task of enabling such development. Good parents do much more than this, they fiercely protect their children from harm whilst pushing and supporting their position in the world. They operate with a *loving prejudice* which promotes the child's welfare and enables the child to develop positive self-regarding sentiments. The child who is cared for by professional people is subjected to a different form of care, based more upon logical discipline than loving prejudice, more upon expediency and compromise than passion. Professionals who operate within the context of 24-hour-care settings are often faced with the practical task of having to respond to a particular problem because it is their professional duty to do so. Too often professionals do not know what to do, but feel that they must do it anyway, and the resulting action has less to do with the child's needs than with the professional's own motives. Although the establishment of discipline may cover the member of staff's need to maintain professional control, and the resolution of problems may remove the problem from the professional's workload, unless such actions are based upon the concepts of fairness and appropriateness for both the child and the member of staff, one will inevitably feel abused by the other. The need to protect the child from the professional indulgences of those staff who are compelled to affect the child's life either out of a desire to preserve institutional or personal control, or a mistaken sense of professionalism, is an essential part of maintaining the paramountcy principle. Volume 4 makes reference to the need to ensure that 'homes do not attempt to use methods to care for children which require a level of competence, experience and qualification which the staff complement does not, in fact, possess' (1.30). The Utting Report (1991: 36) raises darker issues of institutionalised practices which develop without external scrutiny, involving ingrained cultural attitudes, discriminatory and demeaning attitudes and gender issues.

As professionals do not have all the answers to the problems facing children, it has become a basic canon of the Problem Decelerating Environment that, in most cases, no action is better than wrong action. Unless someone is at serious risk, the member of staff who is confronted with a problem which is beyond his or her competence or knowledge should, at best, do nothing, seeking guidance and assistance as soon as it is practically possible to do so. If a problem situation cannot be reduced, care should be taken to ensure that it is not intensified by a precipitous intervention.

All interventions into the child's life, especially when intervention is aimed at disturbed or disruptive behaviour, should contain three basic elements, an Objective, a Relevance to the child, and a Deceleration of problems (ORD).

1) The intervention should have an *objective* or clearly recognised purpose. Staff should know exactly what it is they are attempting to do and how they can best achieve that end.
2) The intervention should be *relevant* to the child, that is, the action taken must first and foremost be of benefit to the child.
3) The intervention should attempt to *decelerate* the level of problems facing the child. The level of stress, anxiety, anger, grief or confusion should be reduced for the child as a consequence of the intervention, and not increased.

Consistent staff response patterns can only operate if the organisational environment gives permission for them to do so. If, when handling aggressive youngsters, a member of staff is told, 'If you don't know what to do, step away and give the child space', the instruction can only work if the member of staff feels that the human environment has also given permission for that response. If such behaviour is seen as a sign of weakness by senior staff, colleagues or children, then it will be almost impossible for the member of staff to follow its advice. Some human environments give conflicting and confusing permissions to staff and children operating both official and hidden agendas.

A variety of alternative human environments can be created within the houses or units on one campus, or between different groups of staff. This latter is never more true than when a new Headmaster or Principal takes up post in an established institution. Some staff, perceiving their own position and status as tied up in the old way of doing things, will attempt to maintain the old human environmental influences. Other staff will seize the opportunity for self-development, supporting changes in the human environment vigorously. Although this conflict creates many tensions between groups of staff, the real impact is upon the children.

Providing appropriate staff

There is a legal and a professional requirement to protect children from staff who are deemed unsuitable to care for them. Volume 5, section 3.3.1 requires the thorough checking of all who are employed or who have substantial unsupervised access to children. Managers must check DES list 99 and in all cases, prior to employment of staff, a full positive vetting should be initiated. Managers may do well to remember that they are not only looking to employ someone, they are essentially looking for people who will be primary carers of children. Perhaps managers at interviews should pretend that they are looking for foster parents for their own children. Volume 4 (1.28, 1.29, 1.30) emphasises both the need to employ an appropriate number of competent, experienced and qualified staff in addition to providing a quality of staffing.

A further emphasis has been placed upon the need to provide the opportunity for staff to gain the special expertise and qualifications which they need to carry out the tasks required of them. It is unacceptable to assume that the chaplain, nurse or housemaster's wife are adequately qualified to provide counselling sessions for disturbed children, or that they will be sought by children who wish to share problems or make disclosures of abuse. It is time that the caring task was accorded the high status it deserves by ensuring that only carefully selected, appropriately trained, experienced and qualified staff are charged with the care of the children living away from home.

Personal and institutional stress

Children must be protected from a range of stressors relating to their own history, daily living requirements and relationship expectations. Stress comes from many sources. It is not the serious incidents in life which are necessarily stressful, although such events may be extremely painful, traumatic or invoke profound grief, distress and anguish. It is the intense stream of demands accompanying both traumatic and mundane events which for many are truly stressful. Group-care living offers many opportunities for the injection of stress into children's lives. Lack of privacy and high levels of communality in all areas of life, institutional time scales and timetables, the impersonal nature of domestic and personal hygiene, mandatory involvement in unwanted activities, all combine to create stress in a child's life. Often children are forced to make adaptations, accepting a lack of privacy, enduring intrusions into personal and private routines, tolerating the fact that many basic decisions will be made for them. By doing so they accept, in principle, a level of personal abuse and deprivation. Such acceptance may be the pragmatic consequences of a lack of alternatives, or it may be the consequence of a desire to be accepted both by those who create such situations, and those who also accept such things. Where children are deprived of choice and privacy, a vulnerability to other forms of abuse is enabled.

Children, living in batch-care situations away from home and parents, deprived of privacy and individuality, are placed under stress in many areas. Children under stress become perceptually rigid. They are subject to over-reaction and over-adaptation, repressing natural feelings and losing touch with their own locus of control. The establishment must attempt to reduce stress in its institutional forms by attending to the way in which the emotional and psychological environment is generated. Not only should the physical environment enable privacy and individuality, reducing the excesses of batch living, it should deliberately attempt to reduce the levels of hassle in the child's life. Being able to look after one's clothing appropriately, protecting one's personal possessions from the excessive prying of another child, or one's socks from the ravages of the laundry system, being able to bathe and perform self-care functions in private, are basic rights which, if given up, make it easier to accept other deprivations as they follow on. The absence of such processes are dehumanising and intimidatory and should not be seen as 'character building'.

Feeling secure

Children who live away from home are often severed from their roots at an earlier stage than would normally occur had they remained with their family. Children who live away from their families, especially those who are ostensibly away for most of their childhood, are in danger of losing contact with their own history. Birthdays, anniversaries and special events should be fully and appropriately celebrated. Children should be encouraged to develop an understanding of their own histories and they should be supported in building up a cache of personal possessions, memorabilia, photographs, letters, documents, etc., which can be used as a source of information and a basis for constructing their own personal histories. Communal living must not prevent the children from seeing themselves as unique individuals with unique and accessible histories.

The family has the potential to provide the child with a sense of permanence and belonging. The child, feeling safe and secure in the home, is able to venture out into the world to tackle the next series of developmental tasks, returning for support and guidance as and when required. The establishment must replicate this situation for every child accommodated. Children cannot be bounced through this stage. If the stage is not completed, natural development will not be achieved and developmental tasks will remain unresolved. Children cannot be suddenly expected to cope merely because they now reside in a particular establishment, any more than they should suddenly be expected to grow 12 inches in height or change the colour of their hair.

Security grows from a sense of belonging. Each establishment must develop a deliberate means of 'claiming' the child. This precedes the child claiming the establishment. Its consequence is the enabling and empowering of the child. Claiming is the process by which children are encouraged and enabled to develop feelings of security and belonging. It enables them to come to terms with their own situations in a pragmatic and healthy way whilst allowing them to develop an appropriate knowledge base of social interaction skills. Many children will come to feel that the environment has claimed them when a natural sense of belonging develops, but this is not true for all children. Some children need help in making appropriate adaptations from one environment to another, and in doing so it may be necessary that they come to accept the reality of situations which they have little chance of changing. Although the most difficult adaptation which many children have to make is to accept changes in parental relationships, they must also come to accept that in many things they will be competent but never brilliant. Adapting to personal reality can be painful. Claiming is the beginning of a process which leads to the meeting of important developmental tasks by which children can free themselves to 'move on', both in terms of their own development and maturity, and their own progression through the institution from admission to leaving.

The duality of self

The Problem Decelerating Environment Approach targets the child's concept of self as a key area of attention. The developing child needs to develop and sustain a positive yet realistic identity. The self concept contains a duality of self, the actual self and the ideal self. The *actual self* is that part of the self concept which tells the child what sort of a person he or she is within the various life settings. Part of this picture is based on the individual child's experiences, feelings and emotions, successes and failures, and part is based upon the feedback received from the world around, how others appear to see, react to, accept or reject the child. The *ideal self* is a database of information as to how the self should ideally be. It is created by the child's perception of the ideal, based upon information given by others, including primary adults, peers and society models, and gleaned from television, video and other media forms. Horney (1951: 22) describes this process.

> Each person builds up his personal idealized image from the materials of his own special experiences, his earlier fantasies, his particular needs, and also his given faculties. If it were not for the personal character of the image, he would not attain a feeling of identity and unity.

When the child compares the real self with the ideal self and feels that there is a negative 'match', the result will be a negative self-regarding sentiment, the greater the disparity between the two versions of self, the more negative and painful will be the self-regarding sentiment. If the child compares the two versions of self favourably, feeling that the ideal self is matched in all relevant areas, the self-regarding concept will be positive. Children who live with a group of peers who emphasise success in terms of antisocial behaviour will themselves move towards antisocial behaviour in order to improve their self-regarding sentiments, unless there are opposing values which have meaning and relevance. The highly introspective boy, fearing mandatory sports, experiences not only the fear and anxiety connected with having to do the things which he does not feel able to do, but also suffers the pain of negative self-regarding sentiments as his belief that he is a failure as a sportsman leads to feelings of worthlessness as a person. The child may turn to similarly worthless others who have found themselves in the same dilemma.

Given that all children operate at different levels of introspection and action orientation, their lives and self concepts often cluttered by a range of disturbances, each will approach the task of integration from a different starting point. In most establishments there are unhappy children who are out of phase with the main themes of the establishment. In many cases they have to live with the situation, remaining relatively isolated and stoically unhappy throughout their residence without ever coming to terms with the demands made of them. Others make whatever adaptations they can and learn to make the best of the situation.

Coping with failure

Many disturbed and damaged children coming into residence have failed in their living situations, often unable to trust others, form reciprocal relationships, or take on personal commitments. Often they resent involvement in the routine institutional daily activities which initially appear to emphasise their plight, but ultimately come to provide them with security and protection from the external world (Davison, 1984). Many children, prior to residential care, have failed with spectacular success and attempts to get the children to re-tackle life tasks are preordained to failure. The Problem Decelerating Environment Approach requires that children are offered a wide range of new activities. Some new activities may require a high degree of action orientation, for example, abseiling, climbing, camping, motor-triking, cliff and fell walking, canoeing and rafting, gardening, building, pottery, and enameling. Some new activities require a high level of introspection orientation, for example, discussion groups, counselling sessions, chess, information technology, writing, word-games and quizzes, communication activities, creating a newspaper, drama, and specific artistic tasks including penmanship and video film making. Children feel able to tackle new activities because they are new, interesting and they do not carry a legacy of failure. With help and support from concerned and involved adults the children can achieve good levels of success in the new activities and this impacts strongly upon their self-regarding sentiments. As they develop more positive feelings about themselves, beginning to readjust their concept of an ideal self to include the new areas of involvement, so they become more able to face up to the important life tasks which they have previously avoided. Thus the Problem Decelerating Environment involves the creation of a wide range of totally new experiences which provide opportunities for the children to be successful in areas which have no history for them. Success in the 'new' areas can be used to develop the children's self-regarding sentiments and boost self confidence and self appreciation. This in turn becomes a base for tackling the old areas of functioning with a new and far more positive expectation of success. Abseiling can promote school attendance and initiate positive involvement with authority figures. Canoeing and climbing can stimulate success in relationships, and pottery and horticulture can lay the foundations for success in future work environments. A range of activities should be designed to provide for the whole child, developing both introspective and action-oriented-based skills. A positive human environment firstly encourages the individual, and then permits the group to benefit from this. (Rather than encouraging the group and hoping that all the members will fulfil their individual potential.) In all residential establishments, primary adults must actively seek out the children who are in danger of failing and provide appropriate programmes, designed to improve the child's self-regarding sentiments, emphasising the child's all-round welfare.

Enabling the child

The greatest risk to children living in residential care or a boarding environment is the imposition of a state of powerlessness or disenablement. Children should feel safe and secure in their own home. At home with their families they may have some control over the environment, mainly by virtue of the intense and emotional relationships they have with the primary adults who control the environment. They should see their family as enabling them to get the best out of life, promoting their welfare, caring for them when they are ill, protecting them when they feel vulnerable. Children living in residential institutions can be deprived of such relationships. They are often one of many residents, with relatively few adults around to support, protect and care for them. Batch living can restrict the expression of emotions. Here, Horney (1951: 84) may have been offering observations upon the impact of residential and boarding settings.

> The taboo on feelings of tenderness, sympathy, and confidence can be just as great in some neurotics as the taboos on hostility and vindictiveness are in others. These people feel that they should be able to live without any close personal relations, so they believe that they do not need them. They should not enjoy anything; so they believe that they do not care. Their emotional life then is less distorted than plainly impoverished.

The size of the establishment, the number of people resident, the number and status of the staff, the power of the organisation, all combine to disempower the children who often feel as if caught in a one-way torrent against which there is no fighting. The children feel out of touch with home, family and friends and can do little about it. They may be involved in activities which they find unacceptable or distressing but have little access to change for fear of the system, the peer group or the institutional code of practice.

Residential establishments can often be the venue for a range of power relationships. The relationship between staff and children is the one which is most prone to the degradations of power wielding. In power relationships, the more powerful one member becomes, the more disempowered is the other. Members of staff who wield an authoritarian control over children not only emphasise their own control, they emphasise the helplessness of the child (Davison, 1984). In such relationships the child's problems are rarely addressed because the child is unable to find a relevant place to voice them. Too often in power relationships problems are solved by repression and intimidation, even when the powerful one is not aware of this. When the problem ceases to present itself to the member of staff, for the member of staff the problem ceases to be, leaving the child to find another way of seeking resolution. Often the human environments created by the children are themselves the most inflexible and authoritarian, refusing children permission to cope with problems in the more usual and natural ways. Children may soon establish that crying, seeking help from adults or complaining to parents are unacceptable response patterns, whilst toughness, self restraint and aggression are held in high esteem. The environment may support a code of conduct in which the taboo against telling tales is even stronger than the child's drive for self preservation. Children know the value of power relationships and often implement them in a basic and savage manner. The fewer the staff available, and the greater the degree of staff specialisation, the greater the danger that power relationships will be applied inappropriately by children and staff.

Children are not possessions to be structured and organised. They are sentient, emotional, developing people who need support and guidance. They must be enabled to gain control over their own lives in both daily events and long-term planning. Children must exercise their ability to choose, both in areas which are important to them, and those which are traditionally required of them (in the classroom and social settings). They must also have choice in selecting the things that they do. Choice is the great enabler. Often the actual choice made is unimportant, the importance lying in being able to choose. Children give a greater commitment to those things in which they have been involved. The process of 'claiming' is the first step towards individual enablement, encouraging and ensuring the development of feelings of security and belonging, allowing the children to come to terms with their own situations. Children should feel involved in the decisions which have led to their current living and educational arrangements, and they should be part of any future discussions which may subsequently change things. Claiming enables children to tackle developmental tasks, freeing them to 'move on' in terms of their own development and maturity. Giving children a voice in their own lives, be it in choice of friends, activities, food, clothes, contact with others, is to support them in taking the first step towards real independence.

Speaking out

Children who feel able to speak out, having access to the mechanisms which enable them to do so, are at far less risk of assault and abuse than children who are intimidated into accepting the painful and abhorrent as normal and acceptable. Such 'enabled' children are more able to seek help when they need it, to seek advice and support when it is required and to refuse to be involved in those things which they know they should not accept. There are many ways of enabling children to have an influential voice in their own lives. The representations procedures which have emanated from the Children Act offer one venue which can operate at a range of levels, from the informal discussion to formal tribunal. There is, however, a great deal of scope for the development of systems which will enable the child to speak out within the context of normal everyday events. Student councils and committees can be encouraged to share in the monitoring and provision of 'Quality Care Systems', advising and requesting, debating and implementing the changes which are necessary to improve the quality of life. Children can be involved in decisions about their own lives including choice of activities, changes in living arrangements and contact with others. Children must see that their feelings and wishes are important and are taken into account even when the decisions are not what the child would wish. Where problems occur, children should feel that they are able to give their side of the story, openly and honestly, knowing that it will be taken into consideration.

It is important that children have access to those who are in a position to take their problems seriously, offering care, advice and support, obtaining justice or protection and where necessary initiating change. This requires that the child has choice as to which person they wish to see. Volume 4 suggests that although one member of staff may take responsibility for the individual child, children should be able to develop relationships with other staff members with whom they have regular contact, and must not be forced to form special relationships with staff who are not of their choosing. In the *Practice Guide* (Department of Health (1991)) are similar comments. Section 6.19 emphasises the need to make available a range of staff who can listen to children, allowing children to turn to any member of staff who they feel they can trust, adding,

> This has implications for the way in which house staff listen to other staff who may have important things to say about children and for the need to include them, as appropriate, in pastoral discussions.

Children should have access to a range of people with whom they can discuss and communicate areas of concern. Independent visitors and advocates are a welcome addition, and will no doubt provide a worthwhile service, but for children living within the constraints of a peer code of practice which does not encourage passing information to outsiders (in some cases the staff are seen as outsiders), the decision to take such a route will create additional stress and create problems which may prove to be insurmountable. Paradoxically the establishments which enable children to speak out freely and openly will produce the greatest volume of complaints including utilisation of the representations and advocacy procedures, whilst the establishments in which children most need to speak out will continue to produce few complaints because of the complaint-retarding mechanisms which exist within such repressive environments.

Democratisation

The aim of every establishment must be to create an environment in which all members share equal levels of respect, integrity and opportunity, having access to the promotion of individual rights. This will reduce the 'us and them' culture and eventually lead to a high level of democratisation for all. Staff must be empowered to fulfil their obligations to care for the children but in turn, staff must empower the children, enabling them to grow in a healthy, purposeful and secure way. The creation of genuine democratisation does not reduce all to the same level, rather it gives every one access to the same human and individual rights whilst ensuring that value is accorded to the different roles that each person or group of persons play within the institution. Many staff will remain unconvinced of a move which goes against the accepted and established relationship structures which have worked so well, for so long, for them.

Handling risks and making decisions

Both the staff and the 'system' must learn to accept failure as a valuable tool which can enable a child's positive individual development. When children have 'failed' in the context of an activity, there is a force which tries to stop the activity occurring again. When older pupils, allowed to go down to the local village during an evening, come back under the influence of alcohol, there is a force which presses for the banning of pupils having access to the local village in the evening as if the problem lay in the activity and not in the way it was handled. The activity is relevant to the children's development and one which they can mostly handle. They will not learn to cope with potential problems by having the whole activity removed from their sphere of involvement (Davison, 1990:

18–21). Attention should concentrate upon improving the 10 per cent of the activity which went wrong, whilst preserving the 90 per cent which was successful, rather than throwing everything away in a sense of failure. It must be recognised however, that banning the activity removes the problem as a problem for staff. The staff and the 'system' must learn to cope with problem behaviour in a way which targets long-term aims and objectives and not merely by attending to the immediate reduction of problem outcomes for themselves or others. This requires that thought is given to establishing a range of appropriate aims and objectives for both the child and the establishment, recognising that, 'A hope is not an aim, or, as others have said, "one cannot make an 'is' out of an 'ought'".' (see Patterns and Outcomes, 1991: 65, 2 and 3).

Too often the managers and staff respond to a child's problem by actions designed to meet their own needs or those of the system, rather than attempting to meet the needs of the child (Hall, 1982: 43). The act of punishing children who run away merely punishes the child for returning and not for running away. Punishments make the system operators feel content, having responded 'appropriately' to the rule breaker, and, as a bonus, the punishment may even deter the child from running away again. Although the system has achieved its purpose, the outcome for the child is much different. Whatever unhappy situation stimulated the running away, an unhappier stimulus has taken its place. Surely it is best to attend to the child's problem within the establishment, removing the need to run away, promoting happiness and well-being. Behaviour such as running away is usually functional. Where it fails to reduce the child's problems appropriately, the child will not run away again. If the running away serves a purpose for the child, staff may intervene according to the ORD directive offered previously. If the staff response has a specific objective (stop the running away by removing the problem stimuli), a relevance to the child (the child can see an actual change or can perceive the same problem differently), and a decelerating affect (the child is given time to find alternative and more suitable ways of handling the problem) there is a greater opportunity for success in child-centred terms. If the child feels able to deal with problems by utilising appropriate systems within the establishment, activities such as running away will be rare.

Open and enabling establishments are pro-active, they look for the problems and establish acceptable and appropriate mechanisms by which the child can have the problems addressed. Authoritarian and closed establishments may have a tendency towards being reactive, waiting until the problem occurs and then trying to do something about it. They may, however, have difficulty separating the actual problems from the problems created by the child's attempts to handle the problem. Closed environments are repressive. They react to problems by removing the manifestation of the problem, abandoning the child to cope with the problem in a way which does not irritate or involve a cost to the system.

The establishment which promotes a positive human environment, seeking to enable all who live and work within its domain, striving to nurture positive self-regarding sentiments in each individual member, reflects its position by the quality of care offered. The physical environment should reflect the high level of esteem in which the children are held, ensuring that they receive the best possible care. There is something perverse in the attitude that children who are deprived and made to suffer hardship, be it a short sharp shock or horsehair mattresses and cold showers, will in time become better, more well-adjusted adults. Children who are cared for and made to feel worthwhile are more able to appreciate other people's feelings and needs. Children who are uncertain of the relationship they hold with primary others experience anxiety and stress, and their perceptions become centred upon themselves. Horney (1951: 19) suggests that healthy human relationships involve the ability of one person to move towards, away from, or against the other without jeopardising the quality of that relationship. This facility is not mutually exclusive.

> The ability to want and give affection, or to give in; the ability to fight, and the ability to keep to oneself − these are complementary capacities necessary for good human relations. But in the child who feels himself on precarious ground because of his basic anxiety, these moves become extreme and rigid. Affection, for instance, becomes clinging; compliance becomes appeasement. Similarly, he is driven to rebel or to keep aloof, without reference to his real feelings and regardless of the inappropriateness of his attitude in a particular situation. The degree of blindness and rigidity in his attitude is in proportion to the intensity of the basic anxiety lurking within him.

There is a language of acceptance and personal worth which can be imbibed by children if it is an important and regular feature of the human environment in which they feel safe and secure. There is also a language of violence and power which can be learned. There are serious problems inherent in establishments in which children are left to create their own environmental conditions and language. Children take cues from the surroundings in which they are placed, responding to their environment in part according to their own feelings and in part according to the value which adults appear to attach to it. It is important that living areas are attractive and comfortable, that bedrooms allow privacy and convey a feeling of security and permanence, and leisure activities have adequate and appropriate space. Children's living space is an extension of their own identity and the children should, as far as possible, be involved in choosing the fabrics, designs, colour schemes and furnishings which are to be used in their own rooms. They should be able to personalise their sleeping areas and be able to maintain their private possessions safely and securely.

Controlling care quality

It is probable that, in time, every establishment will have at least one senior person on the staff responsible for monitoring, maintaining and improving the quality of care within the establishment. The person appointed should be an expert in residential care rather than a management, administration or education expert. The appropriate monitoring and assessment of establishment climate requires a relevant and extensive knowledge of residential child care, linking the needs of the children and staff with the aims and objectives of the establishment. Quality of care should be an over-riding principle and not an after-thought or empty gesture.

The opportunity to grow

An integral part of this requirement is the provision of a range of experiences for the children, primary and secondary, physical and intellectual, personal and social, which should serve to create a series of opportunities for individual development and the growth of personal competence. Children should neither be left to make individual adaptations to the demands of personal and social developmental stages alone, nor should they be forced to depend upon peers who are likewise engaged in fundamental development tasks.

The staff contribution

It is to be hoped that over the next few years much effort will be given to the redevelopment of various forms of residential care and education. The false cultural divisions which have fractured the residential provision cannot be expected to stand for ever. The principles which underwrite residential care in its various forms must be shaped into a professional discipline because that is the only way of ensuring that children who live in residential and boarding settings, are both offered every opportunity to fulfil their own unique potential and gain protection from abuse.

Although the task of each establishment may be different in terms of the object function (the reasons which led to the child being placed in the establishment), the core function of each unit (providing the child with normal living and developmental opportunities) must be the same. Each establishment may offer different methods of treatment, care and education, offering different facilities, designed to meet different needs, operating from different religious or historical principles, but the ways in which care and nurture are provided for the children and young people must reflect the same philosophic base and that must be founded upon the philosophy inherent within the Children Act. The Holbrook Group is a professional movement committed to this end.

Maintaining normality

Attempts to improve the children's self-regarding sentiments, the quality of the physical environment and the child's access to personal development opportunities must be supported by the maintenance of a high degree of normalisation within the daily routines and activities. Attention to ways in which the child can participate in decisions affecting self must look towards establishing an ability to cope with normal life demands in later life. The child's needs must be met on a total basis. Plans for the child must be as relevant to the child in the long term as they are on an immediate and short-term basis. The child must be addressed as a whole person, care and attention being given as much to the normal non-problematic areas of functioning and development as upon those which are problematic. Ultimately all work undertaken with the child should be directed at enabling the child to move out into the world under self control and direction in a healthy and socially appropriate manner.

Achieving independence

The move towards independence begins the moment the child enters the establishment. Through the process of claiming, the child must first learn to be dependent, for it is only through dependency that the child can progress to inter-dependence and then to independence. Dependence involves trusting primary others, feeling safe to challenge and question them, feeling safe to make mistakes and come for advice, or to seek support when trouble abounds. Dependence is having primary adults upon whom the child can model his own behaviour, lay down the foundations of attitudes, prejudices and beliefs on a range of issues, and upon whom the child can depend for protection when the world turns snarling, threatening to inflict hurt or deprivation. Serious questions must be addressed to the larger establishments where relatively large numbers of children are dependent upon relatively few adults. If the child does not have appropriate access to primary-role adults, how can a state of dependence be reached? Children do not benefit from a total dependency relationship with other children who are also struggling to meet different or similar developmental tasks. A dependency relationship with primary adults helps the child to move out into the world on his or her own terms, knowing full well that when problems occur someone will be there to provide support, advice and assistance. As the child takes on more interactions with the world, as of his or her own right, the move towards independence begins. Although it is important that the child learns the skills associated with achieving personal and social independence, social skills alone do not enable independence. Children who are successful within establishments are not necessarily successful in the world outside. Children leaving care are often vulnerable and unable to cope with the demands which are made of them. Many individuals leaving boarding school to enter university feel just as vulnerable and confused. Patterns and Outcomes (1991: 9) observes, 'Leaving care for independence is a crisis which brings to the surface past deficits in care and attainment.'

The task of enabling independence must be at the core of all work undertaken with the child in residential care and boarding. Children

120

who return to their own homes in the community or move on into the vastly different structures of higher education having developed a genuine independence will be more able to resist immersion in relationship difficulties, or fall foul of antisocial influences and anti-personal activities. Children who have been enabled in their move towards independence will have gained a realistic perspective of their own abilities and life expectations and as a result will be able to lead a happier and more fulfilled life. This is a crucial element of caring and is central to the 'alternative to parenting' task. The concepts offered within the Problem Decelerating Environment Approach can assist in meeting these tasks.

CHAPTER 7

Communication Need
Martin Callow

Introduction

The need for good communication between all those who are involved in a residential-care community, not just the carers but also the cared for, is a principle which is emphasised in the Children Act. By ensuring good communications, it may be possible to ensure that children are properly looked after and fully protected against those who might take advantage of them. However, communications between children and adults are complicated by many factors, some of which are to be explored in this chapter.

The organisational structure, an adult's perspective

As organisations become larger, the complexity of maintaining a single or limited number of purposes, requires a greater formalisation of structure, hence the epithet 'organisation'. Members of the group will be required to regularise their behaviour so that the aims of that organisation can be achieved. In larger organisations a division of responsibility will emerge, and a hierarchical structure will tend to develop from this. Once the framework of the social organisation is established, it can have a profound effect on the interactions of the people within it. The organisation itself will define and justify certain positions or ranks, necessary to maintain integrity and direction, and these will then become perpetuated regardless of the individuals who may temporarily occupy them. For example, the school will have a headteacher, the diocese, a bishop, and the street gang, a leader. When the current incumbent moves on for whatever reason, a suitable successor is sought, not to replace the personality, but to occupy the role.

The concept of role is an important one. Goffman (1969) points out that the role, as described here, goes beyond the prescribed duties of any particular position. It also includes the expectations of others within the same social organisation in terms of behaviour and interaction to other members of the group. In this sense, roles are essentially static and prescribed within an organisation (Mead, 1934; Linton, 1945) and individuals will move in and out of them, occupying both role and position. A principal or headteacher of a school may be expected to act in a powerful and assertive way, and will be judged by the staff by the extent to which the role expectations are fulfilled.

There is a strong link between the concept of roles and that of hierarchies and power structure. The role that an individual might play within a social organisation can be more of a function of relative position within it, and the power that position confers. In the armed forces the rank is clearly displayed on the uniform so that there can be no ambiguity about the role that each individual has to play. Observe the interactions in a hospital casualty waiting area for example and it is not difficult to tell the doctors from the patients, not only from their dress, but because they are acting in a different way. Role and power is also manifest in more subtle ways. Look at the arrangement of the seats in a church or a classroom, and the messages about whom is in charge and where the power lies is obvious, even without any one being present in the room (Hall, 1959). The way that people react to one another within an organisation may be more a function of their relative positions rather than any personality factor.

The way in which the various parts of an organisation interact with each other gives rise to a concept called organisation climate (Chapter 7). A simplistic description can be drawn from that experience obtained within minutes of entering a place; the feelings of chaos or order, efficiency, friendliness, warmth or aloofness. It is another important factor which has an effect on the interactions of the people working within it.

Challenging the assumptions

The adult world of work can be influenced by its organisation structure. Those within it can be considered to be position occupiers, and therefore role players. The way in which people respond to others is a function of several factors including position, power and the organisational climate. When residential-care organisations which cater for children are studied, it is dangerous to assume that role and power structure only involve the adults. It is important for the adults to realise that they enter the structure on a professional basis, and for them it is a place of work. For children the situation is different, it is primarily a place to live. It cannot therefore be presumed that children are some kind of raw material waiting to be converted into something else; an undergraduate, an adult or a law-abiding citizen. The Children Act requires adults to treat the children as responsibilities with a much more active part to play in their own development. The Act in reality, begins to challenge some of these assumptions often made by adults and requires us to try to understand the social organisation from the child's perspective.

The social organisation, a child's view

Most people carry out their everyday activities as members of one group or another. The three most common groups, the ones which are the most influential in our daily lives, are those of family, friendships and work (Argyle, 1969). Children enter our social organisation on a different basis from the adult. The children's world cannot therefore be considered just an extension of that familiar to the adult. To begin to understand how children fit into the social organisation, one must look at the group systems which have most significant influence on them, those being their family and friendship groups.

We are all born into family groups and owe our current existence and survival to the successful functioning of them. The nuclear family, comprising parents and their children includes among its functions that of protecting and developing children until they are sufficiently independent to be integrated into the wider social environment. The bonding between parent and child is naturally intensely strong, particularly in the early years when the child is totally dependent on the parent. The interactions of family life, between child and parents, and with other members of the nuclear group, brothers, sisters and perhaps other close relatives, enable the child to learn to cope with the contingencies and crises of daily life. The emotional support the immediate family provides is of crucial importance. It is important to examine the role structure here, as the interaction between parent and child will have a recognised distribution of power, which is worth further consideration. Children learn and accept from the very earliest age that adults are bigger and stronger, that they are wiser, and to be trusted. The mutual acceptance of this arrangement can be very useful in the child's development. It is used, for example, to enable a parent to control his or her children, and for teachers to control and give learning tasks to children in school. The ease with which we accept this arrangement is such that it is almost sub-conscious and unchallenged. As well as recognising the necessity of this, it is important to be aware that it is the same mechanism that also leaves the children vulnerable to abuse by adults.

Friendship groups are of great importance to children and these will gradually replace some of the functions of family, particularly during adolescence. The friendship group gradually becomes a major agency through which children can make sense of their personal environment, and becomes a main forum for dealing with the contingencies and crises of life. Groups of children have been observed working as part of pupil co-operatives at school (Measor and Woods, 1984), becoming members of ruler-lending and colour-pencil-sharing fraternities that enable them to survive the school day without getting into trouble. Cribbing their friends' homework on the bus and other such activities, show how vital these friendships are to children. The friendship groups are also important in allowing children to make sense of their social surroundings and in formulating some model of predictability. The routine swapping of experiences of their daily lives in the playground, exchanging information on how they were treated by certain teachers and their parents, enables them to form some picture of how to react in the next encounter. Interchanging this information can also inform them of matters such as their parents reaction to their smoking, having their ears pierced or using make-up. It can be of vital and overriding importance to be part of the normal interacting friendship groups. It is possible that friendship groupings have an even greater importance to those children who are in residential care. In such a setting, they provide the basis of the day-to-day continuous interaction that has to substitute for much of the emotional support normally associated with the family group.

Conformists, messers and knife-edgers

Children's interactions can become very finely tuned to the demands of the social situations they are experiencing. For example, physical prowess in boys, being regarded as macho and strong, the desire to be attractive in girls, being clever, and having an interest in the opposite sex can become overriding concerns in adolescence. Conformists, those who remain true to the adult values, are in danger of losing their 'street credibility'. These will include the 'swots' and 'goody-goodies' who can be disliked by many children. Conversely those who deviate too far the other way are also in danger of losing ground with their peer-group identity. Over-use of physical strength could collect the label of 'bully', while over-emphasising sexual attractiveness could gain the child the label of 'tart' or 'slag'.

Deviance from the norms by too great a degree is something to be avoided, especially when it can draw public reproof from adults such as parents or teachers. Therefore children need to keep a safe and acceptable measure of conformity to appease the adults, but at the same time exhibit enough bravado to be accepted by the peer groups. In order to achieve this delicate balance, children use a strategy very aptly described as 'knife-edging' (Measor and Woods, 1984). It describes that behaviour in children that makes them careful of not appearing over-intelligent, like a swot, but at the same time not giving the impression of being stupid or thick, of not wishing to appear to be a goody-goody, but not being associated too strongly with the 'messers'. The art is to gain just enough profile, giving the right messages to both the peer group and the adults such as parents and teachers, without being labelled in a detrimental way. Far from being an 'average', it ought perhaps to be considered as a very calculated position for children to adopt.

From this quite different set of pressures children also begin to develop sets of rules and roles which have an effect on their ability to communicate with adults.

Towards a model of interaction

What has been described so far is two rather different groups of people, adults and children, both preoccupied in their own social settings. They are groups which co-exist in residential settings rather than appear as a natural continuation of each other. This raises the questions about the assumptions which may prevail in residential care. For example, do the adults assume that the children naturally occupy the opposite end of the power spectrum without real rights and with little say in the way in which they are treated? After all it would be quite natural for this to occur given the conditioning of childhood and parenthood. The difference in status, and the differing priorities that both adults and children have is likely to result in difficulties of communication. To put this into sharper relief, imagine the improbability of a child asking his or her foster parent, headmaster or head of care unit, to borrow their telephone to contact 'Childline'. This perhaps unlikely example does serve to illustrate the point that the differing power and status of the people involved can present a problem in the communication process between children and adults. It is not necessarily as straightforward as one might imagine.

However, the issue remains that in order to care effectively for the children, the two systems must be able to communicate with each other effectively, and methods or devices must be found to enable those children to make their feelings known freely to adults. To administer 'care', in a professional sense, without actively listening to the feedback of those who are receiving it, can be considered a rather cosy complacency. If no complaint is received about care practice, can it be safely assumed that it is appropriate, and that it addresses the needs of young people? Cases such as that of Crookham Court clearly demonstrate that there are dangers in the concentration of all the power in the hands of too few people, and that there are difficulties of those who were in care to make known their feelings about the way they were being treated.

Before attempting to understand any system which may be used to improve the channels of communication between children and adults, it will first be necessary to understand the ways in which children actually respond to those around them, particularly within residential settings. The way in which children express their anxiety about those things that cause them distress is of particular importance in this discussion. It is vital to understand to whom they are able to make disclosures of unhappiness, and under which circumstances they can feel confident to do so. Whether drawing from our own experience, or from observing those children who are in our care, it seems that the things which children perceive as being important can often seem trivial and unimportant to the adults around them. The adult reaction will depend on how the adults perceive the importance of the subject. Reaction to the problem can also depend on the position the adult holds in relation to the child, and therefore the role which that person will be expected to play. Any model of interaction involving children needs to take these factors into account. It may also provide the basis for examining the social nature of our own residential care environments from a child's point of view.

As the Children Act requires, it would seem appropriate to start by placing the child in the centre of the model, and then to examine how other people, both children and adults interact with this child (see Figure 4). By examining some typical behaviours, it is perhaps possible to build around this central personality, a set of concentric circles, within which we can map these other people according to the way they help that child cope with the worries and anxieties of life. It may then be possible to develop a framework to understand how the Children Act attempts to address the issue of communication need.

The inner circle – close friends

This inner circle represents those children who are closest to the child concerned. They will be the best friend, the brother or sister and members of the peer group. In normal circumstances a very high degree of interaction will take place within this circle and, through this, a fund of knowledge, a common experience is built up over time between those children. The importance of this collective experience is that it can be drawn upon by the group members to help cope with and solve many problems, particularly the minutiae of daily life. For the children who are in residential care communities, away from the direct emotional support provided by the family, these groups perform perhaps an essential role in this respect (Callow, 1988). They allow the group to absorb the ups and downs of daily life, and they provide the support necessary to keep emotions in proper perspective. It must be realised that because of the close proximity of the members of this circle, and the nature of children's peer groups, that not every problem can be handled by close friends. The importance of peer relationships to children have been discussed and any disclosure which by its nature might threaten or undermine the credibility of a child within the group is likely to be hidden behind a protective front. Anything that the child might feel ashamed of, such as physical or sexual abuse, is unlikely to be disclosed to close friends. As Goffman (1959) clearly showed, the exposure of the real self in such close communities is fraught with difficulties.

This inner circle is characterised by the absence of adults, and thus the absence of any authority structures, either parental or

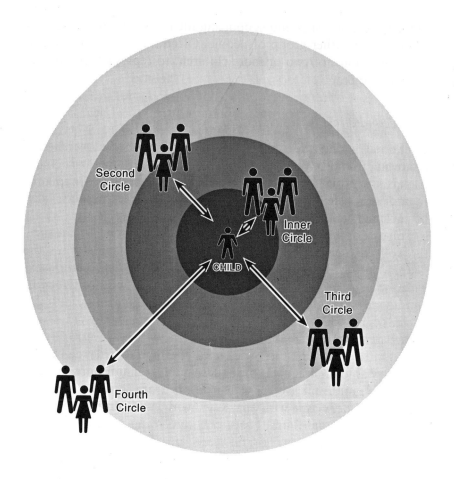

Figure 4   Interactions

institutional. The matters that are discussed within this inner circle, and how solutions are perceived, are 'safe' from adult interference, and consequently the child retains a large degree of control over the options and actions to be taken.

> 'I haven't done my English homework, what am I going to do?'
> 'You can copy mine if you like.'

The choice between bluffing the teacher, copying the homework or skipping the lesson all rest with the child facing the problem. Thus, this inner circle of friends provides a vital function, and has much value in dealing with many minor matters. It also has the important function of discussing and supporting the possibility of taking any problem to another group of people. Often this takes the form of 'the delegation', of two or more children, to represent the worries of one of them.

The second circle — other friends

Contained within the second circle are the other more slightly removed friends, the older brother or sister, perhaps older friends. Significantly it can include some adults. Chaplains, sanatorium sisters, youth club leaders and some teachers, may be included in this circle. The child may use this group directly to solve certain problems, or may have been guided to them by the collective wisdom of closer friends. What characterises the people, both children and adults in this group, is their relationship with the structures of authority. In a family unit, authority can be considered to be held by the parents, in residential communities, it could be by the houseparent, and in a placement, by a foster parent. Thus the second circle person is one who is not directly in authority, but could be in contact with authority figures if necessary. This relationship provides room to manoeuvre.

It is an important group, which differs from the inner circle in that it is a more powerful structure, with more options open to it, but at the same time it does not involve an authority figure. Greater experience, a wider knowledge of possible outcomes, and increased power in both the physical and emotional senses are the reasons why these people may be sought out. The adults who are targeted in this group will probably not have a direct emotional or institutional role to play in the child's life, and therefore do not have placed upon them the pressure to act in an authoritarian role. They can be used by the child to gain adult help and advice, or to provide a sounding board to find out how other, more directly involved adults such as the parents may react. In this respect this group becomes an extremely vital channel of communication.

The children still retain much of the control over the interactions at this state. The adults who are chosen by the children will have been perceived as having some sympathy with them and their culture, and will have possibly been chosen from the corporate fund or peer-group knowledge. As well as those already mentioned there may be other adults within the care system who have the ability to develop the 'cultivation of the middle ground' (Measor and Woods, 1984). These may include cleaning ladies, dinner ladies, gardeners or any other person working in close proximity to children. Any adults who have some authority within the system can also occupy this middle ground, but whether they do will be a function of their own personality and their ability to 'act out of role' at times. Adults who do occupy this role need to be aware of the dangers of emotional over-involvement which can lead to complex and undesirable relationships.

Unfortunately it is not always possible to guarantee that for any child there will be a natural recourse within this circle to one or any of the adults in it. The selection of these people is often a consequence of personality and availability. The large number of children who contact agencies such as Childline clearly demonstrates both the importance and the necessity of communication to this level, and the fact that it is either absent or not obvious to many children in residential care.

The third circle – concerned adults

Some problems or anxieties can, from the child's point of view, only be solved by a more powerful and authoritarian set of people. The third circle therefore contains the first of a series of adults who possess a more responsible and therefore more powerful role. Parents, foster parents and houseparents are typical 'concerned adults' with close emotional links with the child. It is actually because of this more direct involvement, either emotionally, or through being in loco parentis, or both, that they are not necessarily used to resolve an anxiety at an earlier stage. It could be said that one of the roles of the 'go-betweens' in the previous group is to enable children to protect the relationships with those with direct responsibility for their welfare. For example, is it likely for a young girl who thinks that she may be pregnant to discuss this first of all with her parents? Children can bring disclosures of worry either directly, or as a result of advice from their friends, their peers or another adult friend. Sometimes a child will bring a friend along for moral support when making the initial approach.

Direct contact with the concerned adults can be made for several reasons. One is that the child is using this group as a substitute for discussing matters that would normally be part of the interaction with children in closer circles. Such children are often socially isolated from their peers and they are using these adults in this way as a substitute for the co-operative support normally gained from friendship groups. Unfortunately this can easily become an irritation to the adults, because they are being used 'out of role' and it can often gain a child the label of 'attention seeker'. Another reason for a direct approach is with a problem, which, if disclosed to a closer more personal group could damage the self esteem of the child with his or her friends. The importance of maintaining credibility with the peer group is of paramount importance to most children. Direct approaches of this nature can be considered to be a call for help, a request for action. It is important that this is recognised by the adults who receive these anxieties at this level, as they will have been chosen because of their ability, through position and power, to act. Consequently these 'concerned adults' can be approached because of their position rather than their personality. Before, it was suggested that 'close friends' and 'other friends' were used because it was not necessary to involve the 'concerned adults' or to avoid direct confrontation with them, leaving most of the choice of possible outcomes with the child. Once action is invoked by these more powerful adults, the control tends to shift away from the child. The child then has less involvement with the decisions being made on his or her behalf, a danger stressed in the Children Act.

Problems do exist with interactions between children and the 'concerned adults' for several reasons. Whereas the 'concerned adults' will, because of the responsibility vested in them, have status and power either in the family or community, the difference in status in relation to the child can inhibit communication. Children may be too frightened with the way the adults may react, and afraid that they might be punished in some way. They may be too embarrassed to communicate directly, or they may simply lack the self confidence to make an approach. Being in a position to act can also be a barrier to receiving the information from those who need support.

The fourth circle – institutional adults

This circle of people will be the most distant from the child, and are likely to have little direct contact, although they may have responsibility. This will be the sort of people that the 'concerned adults' may use to resolve problems that need appropriate and perhaps particular assistance. This may take the form of expertise and involve people such as doctors, social workers, psychiatrists or counsellors, or it may take the form of greater power such as that vested in policemen or headteachers. The common factor will be that they are official and therefore people of greater influence and representatives of wider social structures. It is because of this that they are much more fixed in their role and much more bound by codes of practice. Thus their actions will tend to reflect the expectations of that role. They will be perceived and expected by the children to act procedurally rather than to be responsive to the individual, and will seem to be too far away to be of any use. Ironically these are the very people that are able to take actions to help children directly in major concerns, such as in cases of abuse or neglect, where action involves mobilising other agencies. Clearly for these reasons, this group represent a very necessary part of the care provision and needs, despite the differences in status, to be accessible to children.

Overview of the model

It should not be assumed that those people who interact with and care for children are assigned to particular and immutable orbits, and that it is impossible for them to adopt more than one role. It is quite feasible for an adult to be a friend in one encounter, and authority figure in another. Parents for example may change role, particularly in those situations where the child is resident away from home. What is important, however, is the way in which the children perceive those people around them, because this will affect their interactions with them. If for example a carer felt that he or she was a friend of a child, but the child considered the carer part of the authority structure, that adult would be precluded from certain types of disclosure. A starting point for an analysis of our own care practices would be to locate the position we ourselves occupy and to see if each child in our care has recourse to all other possible outlets and that there are people in each circle who can be contacted by them (Figure 5).

Communication need and the Children Act

Children are acute observers of adult interactions and adult inter-actions with other children. It is through observation that most children, with reference to their friends, siblings and peer group, may identify the key people and the roles they perform. It is quite important for each child to know which adult to approach with a given problem for the best solution to be found. There is evidence to support the idea that certain problems, because of their nature, will have a tendency to involve particular sets of people.

Analysts of data collected by Childline reveals that there are indeed patterns relating the nature of the problem, and the people that the child has confided in (La Fontaine and Morris, 1992). This would suggest that it is important that each child has some form of direct communication to all parts of the care network to alert others of any distress that is being experienced. This is perhaps more significant for those children who are placed in care away from their parents. It becomes incumbent on those who are responsible for children in residential care to ensure that each child does actually have a full range of communication pathways open so that the care process can be effective. One function of the model may be to form a simple guide to analyse our own institutions or organisations, however large or small, to ascertain whether each child within it is fully supported in this way.

It is also apparent that the organisational hierarchy itself has an important function in the care process. It offers a range of power systems so that the correct degree of emphasis can be applied to each situation to achieve the best solution to the problem. Not only is it important that the adults who have care responsibility are aware of their own relative position in the system in the eyes of the children, but they need also to be sympathetic to the reasons why children might be making disclosures to them personally. This will be particularly important where the person concerned can occupy more than one role. It is crucial that the adult who is approached is sensitive to which role the child is expecting. The wrong response from the adult can be devastating for the child.

The Children Act responds to the needs of children to have as complete a range as possible, of mechanisms through which they can make their feelings known. It requires those who are responsible for the care of children to provide these mechanisms. It sets out to overcome the barriers caused through differences in relative position and status between adult and child. Any distress, anxiety or complaint about the way in which the children are treated, can therefore be expressed in some way, and solutions found. What is of primary importance is that the Act sets up a series of open 'permissions' for the children to make direct contact with the

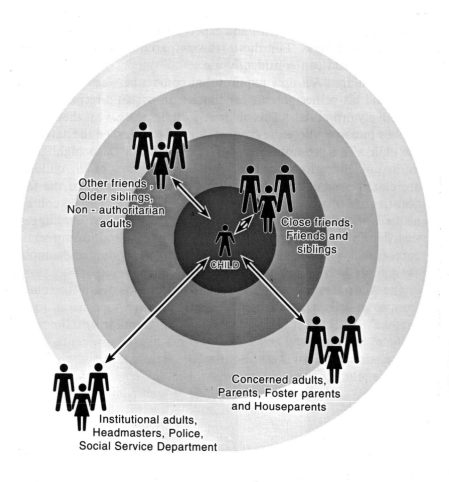

Figure 5   Interaction model

appropriate level in the care system. The Children Act attempts to make provision for fuller communication links through the guidelines for contacts with parents and relatives, the complaints procedures, and the requirements for each child to have recourse to an independent listener.

Contacts with parents

Parents, adults with parental responsibility and other close relatives, can provide vital links with the child in care. In the model parents are shown as authoritarian figures in a 'concerned' role. However parents are in many cases, a group of adults in whom the children can place their trust and expect a supportive response when they are in distress. For these reasons parents form connections which the child can confidently use.

The Children Act now requires that contact between the child in care, and his or her parents (or those with parental responsibility) be actively promoted.[1] This obviously carries the caveat that it only applies in cases where the contact does not prejudice the safety of the child. The promotion of parental contact is also highlighted in the guidelines for boarding schools where most of the children are placed primarily for educational reasons. Mindful of the fact that there is often an immediacy in the need for a child to contact his or her parent when in distress, the guidelines further suggest that there should be facilities to ensure that children can maintain contact with parents, relatives and friends in private, for example, by suitably located payphones.[2]

The Act states very clearly that communications with the family form a vital link between adults and children which needs to be encouraged. The Act also requires that local authorities, boarding schools, hospitals and other residential care establishments, listen to the parents of children who may be distressed in some way, so that the appropriate action can be taken.

The Complaints Procedure

The significance of the Complaints Procedure lies in three principle areas: its role in the social organisation as a form of communication; its importance in being recognised as a procedure; and its function in ensuring that the carers become accountable to those who are being cared for.

The Complaints Procedure tries to ensure that there will always be a route through which information from children who may be requiring help can reach those adults who have the power to provide the necessary solutions. The existence of a Complaints Procedure is a recognition that the differences in status between those adults who have this power, and the children who require help, is too often so great that it can inhibit any contact between the two. The Guidlines (Volume 4) state that:

> Children and others making representatives including complaints should have access to a procedure which provides them with an opportunity to make representations and complaints about, and

challenge decisions made in relation to services provided to them. (paragraph 5.11)

This establishes the right to make the contact if it is thought to be necessary. Of equal importance is that such a procedure should be accessible to the children.[3]

The Complaints Procedure attempts to legitimise links from the centre to the periphery of the model, providing the child with direct communication to the powerful adults. The formalisation of this into a procedure has an important function too. Not only does it establish a clear set of ground rules so that a child can communicate directly with those adults, but it also establishes a 'permission' to make those representations. One of the cosy complacencies that adult carers may have is that the 'permission' to register any disquiet or anxiety about the way in which a child is treated is already inherent within the care system. There may be the assumption that because of the actual presence of adults in proximity to the children such information is bound to surface. This disregards the fact that there are many factors which will put children off discussing their anxieties with those 'concerned adults'. In reality the 'permission' to be critical of the way in which they are cared for, may not actually exist. The Complaints Procedure sets up that 'permission', enabling all children to communicate to any level, and to be able to include only those whom the child wants to involve. In this respect it allows the child some degree of control over the possible events that may follow.

A procedure which is understood and accepted by all parties concerned is legitimised as a form of communication. It allows the child to express any disquiet which may have been difficult to disclose to a 'closer person', particularly where it might impose a strain on the relationship. Reflecting the need for confidentiality at all stages is also an important element. The degree of control this gives the child may make all the difference in giving the child the self confidence to use the procedures.

Effectively, this changes the balance of power between the children and those with direct responsibility for them. The Complaints Procedure allows the children, and any advocate for them to raise questions about the quality of care they experience. The Procedure ensures that children in care are no longer powerless.

The independent listener

The description of the role of the independent listener is a recognition that for full and effective communication, certain adults
must become part of the 'other friends' circle quite close to the
child. In the model these were described as non-authoritarian,
active cultivators of the middle ground, and sometimes the
go-between person. The independent listener is an adult, who,
on behalf of the local authority or residential care establishment,
attempts to fulfil this role.[4] Here the Act recognises the idea that
children need to have an adult, in whom they have trust, who will
act on their behalf if necessary, and furthermore, that if these
people are not naturally available, then they must be provided.
The importance for the adult 'other friend' to function in a
particularly non-authoritarian manner, so that they can provide
an outlet for certain types of anxiety, was outlined in the model.
There is a recognition within the guidelines of the Children Act,
that the role of these adults ought to be different from that of the
more 'concerned adults'.[5] It satisfies a communication need which
exists because of the possible difficulties that can be experienced
between the children and those adults most closely involved with
them. The term independent is also significant here in this respect.
Any connection with what may be perceived as authority by the
child will be open to misinterpretation and lack of real trust. The
independent listener must be seen to be completely outside the
authority structure.

Whilst the creation of independent listeners can be considered to
be slightly artificial, in that it is a created rather than a naturally
evolved liaison, it does attempt to ensure that all children who are
in care, have access to this type of communication. Also important
in this respect are the telephone Help Lines such as Childline. These
provide another mechanism for children at this level, using the
counsellors at the end of a telephone as the independent adults.[6]

Summary

Although it appears quite obvious to most of us that adults and
children observe their social environments in different ways, it
would seem important to reflect on these positions when addressing
the issue of communication between the two groups. Adults come
into residential care as professionals, and we have the tendency

to position ourselves according to the rank and status we hold in our working environment. The children who come to live in such environments have a tendency to be assigned the lowest rank status, which has an effect on communications. It would seem important to recognise that the existence of this status difference makes it difficult for children to articulate their personal anxieties to adults.

Whereas the social world of children in residential care is contiguous with the adult world, it is not necessarily a continuation of it. The child's social world has a much greater emphasis on the interactions of friendship and peer groups. These groupings have great importance to children in providing emotional and moral support and in developing strategies for coping with events which affect their lives. Friendship interactions assume even greater importance for those children who are resident away from home, where they are needed to replace some of the functions of family life. Esteem within the peer group therefore assumes great significance and this factor becomes a powerful determinant in communication between the children and others around them. Children would seem to be very conscious of how certain disclosures may affect their self image, and they tend to make preservation of their peer credibility the highest priority. There would appear to be some rules of engagement determining what can be disclosed to whom.

The model attempts to incorporate these factors into a structure, which provides the basis for further discussion. By placing the child in the centre of the model, other people are mapped according to their typical interaction pattern. Although the model is not regarded as definitive, it can function as a common starting point for the analysis of communication in our own care practices. It is possible to suggest that for full and effective communication between the child and all those with care responsibility direct links with each typical group of people involved in welfare is desirable.

Finally it is clear that the Children Act, through its guidelines on communication need, attempts to ensure that for all children in care all these routes of communication are available. The Children Act has two main functions in this context: firstly it brings the problems of communications with children to the attention of those adults who have care responsibility for them; and, secondly, it legitimises the ways in which some of the barriers to communication can be overcome.

Notes

All notes refer to *Guidance and Regulations*.
1 Volume 4 paragraph 4.9
2 Volume 5 paragraph 3.7
3 Volume 5 paragraph 3.11
4 Volume 4 paragraphs 6.13 and 6.35
5 Volume 4 paragraph 6.40 and volume 5 paragraph 3.11
6 Volume 5 paragraph 3.11

CHAPTER 8

The Impact of the Psychological Environment in Residential Group Care and Educational Settings

Alan J. Davison

A powerful force

The physical environment is a powerful force which shapes the behaviour of all those who live within its boundaries. It is not the only such force. There are other environmental dimensions which are just as powerful in shaping behaviour patterns and determining the degree to which the aims and objectives of any institution are met. Various elements come together to create a unique, emotional and psychological environment. As the physical environment impacts upon all who enter its structures, the emotional and psychological environment exerts a powerful influence upon the residents (Davison, 1985). The greater the time a person spends within the institution, the more significant is the impact of the institution upon that person's functioning.

The virtual closed institution

It is in those establishments which can be categorised as virtual closed institutions that the impact of the emotional and psychological environment is at its most pervasive. Amongst such institutions are 'open' penal institutions, monasteries, army barracks and a wide range of educational and residential institutions for children. Such institutions share a great deal more than just a residential element.

a)   Each offer children an alternative to living at home for a substantial part of their lives.

b)   Each ties together the various aspects of the children's lives. Sleeping, eating, playing, working, schooling and relaxing are all channelled into one environment with essentially one core group of people.

c)   Each institution attempts to work with the children by reducing their contact with the outside community during the periods of residence.

d)   Each institution offers batch living, the process of living, working, and doing in groups, often with an official mode of operation and usually accompanied by an operational range of both actual and unofficial hierarchies, thrusting together disparate groups of youngsters who have no natural connection with each other except the fact that they have, for whatever reason, come together in the same establishment.

e)   Each institution offers an alternative to parenting, promoting alternative forms of caring, and creating alternative opportunities for the maintenance of the children's personal and social development.

f)   Each virtual closed institution lies outside the mainstream way of doing things. It involves only a small number of the general population, and employs groups of adults who are in some way deemed to be especially qualified to tackle the task of caring for and educating a rather special group of people. It is accepted that these staff should offer an expertise, a skills and knowledge base which is either not available to other professional groups or is not required by the people with whom other staff are involved. Often, it is claimed, these staff have a sense of vocation.

It is mainly for these reasons, that this special grouping of residences for children experience the same forms of vulnerability to the impact of the emotional and psychological environment created within their walls.

The human environment

The emotional and psychological environment of an establishment is the source of the organised and applied structures and processes, both formal and informal, which create the basic conditions governing the individual's behaviour as an individual. It is described in many ways, and broken down into a number of different categories.

Gilmer (1974) describes the way in which the social climate offers a permanency which permits those who live within it to behave with a high degree of expectation of the nature of probable occurrences and reactions within it. Moos (1974) describes this as, 'the most critical factor in determining the outcome of treatment'. Litman (1971: 149) described the organisational climate as, 'the summary of the total pattern of expectancies and incentive values that exist in a given organizational setting'. It sets boundaries as to what is acceptable and what is expected, encouraging certain forms of behaviour and discouraging others. It sets the standards by which values are set, individuals valued and relationships enabled. Often its presence is intangible whilst its manifestation is pervasive. It creates an acceptance of certain individuals, their behaviour, and their ideals, whilst condemning other individuals, punishing their behaviour and repressing their ideas. Most of all the emotional and psychological environment informs the individual about self, describing self worth, personal prospects and the individual's place in the order of things. The human environment has the potential for both good and harm. Any differences can only exist between actual establishments and not purely between types of establishments. Knowledge which applies to one residential setting applies to all. Rejections of the lessons learned in one type of establishment, and the rejection of externally sourced knowledge and insight as not being relevant, are amongst the less endearing characteristics of the virtual closed institution. In protecting itself from change and the contamination of its traditional objectives, such establishments create the very conditions by which they will fail to protect their own residents. Whilst it is painful to accept that abuses occur in residential care and boarding environments, it is dangerous to deny that they can occur in specific establishments. Prior to tackling the problem, an acceptance that the problem may potentially exist is required. Volume 5 links the various different residential educational provisions by defining the way in which all children have rights when being cared for away from home (see 2.4.2; 2.4.3).

Countering silence

Nature abhors a vacuum and this is never more apparent than during an analysis of the emotional and psychological environments, terms which will here be conjoined and labelled 'the human environment', for they are both created, and experienced, by the humans who live and interact within the institution. This is not to suggest that all elements are consciously created by humans, far from it. Indecision creates decisions and decisions set up shock waves of consequences which are neither predictable nor readily perceived. Inactivity does not leave empty gaps, nor does it maintain the status quo. Inactivity permits other unplanned and uncontrolled activities to take place.

The abhorrent events of Crookham Court and the Pindown Experience, and the situations which have occurred in Leicestershire and elsewhere, are the consequence of the loathsome actions of a few people whose actions were allowed to grow into a range of activities which became offences against those for whom they were charged with caring. In such cases the human environment either prevented, or failed to enable a level of institutional openness which would have allowed the children to signal their problems to the world. Such offences are detestable, but they happened, and there will be opportunities for them to happen again so long as institutions fail to take account of, control, and positively shape, the totality of the human environment in which they live and work.

A voice for all

An institution which actively encourages the residents to question and complain, and then provides opportunities for children to be involved in both the organisation and the practice of caring, will create children who complain and criticise more often, more forcefully, and more ably than children in institutions which do not permit such outspokenness. It is not in those institutions from which residents can and do regularly complain and criticise that the horrific revelations of consistent and lengthy child abuse emerge. It is in the institutions in which children's behaviour is carefully controlled, children's rights repressed and the children maintained in a state of disempowerment that psychological, emotional, sexual and physical abuse is most able to grow. One should not become overly concerned that children in one school, home or house unit are raising complaints or problems. Rather one should address the problems they are raising openly and appropriately, for as with all life tasks, children have to learn to use complaints and representations procedures appropriately. One should become seriously concerned when children appear to have no complaints. Too often lack of complaint equates with no facility to complain, or the presence of a force which prevents complaints from emerging, be it the consequence of fear and intimidation, the power of ignorance, or a child's reluctance to break the peer group 'code'.

Of equal importance is the need to ensure that staff have a voice and are accorded the same level of support and protection as the children for whom they care. Protection of children in care should not and cannot be achieved by abusing the staff who care for them. Child protection and representation procedures must be designed as much to enable good care practices as to eradicate bad care practices. The development of a professional caring service would be irreparably damaged if the current positive moves to enable and protect children led to a disempowerment and further disillusionment of the staff who care for children living away from home. There is a danger that too much attention is focused upon being seen to support children's rights and not enough attention to ensuring that children's rights are actually linked to children's needs.

Perhaps the strongest feature of the human environment is that it gives permission for things to happen. Its weakest feature is that the permission which is given is not underwritten by morality, ethics or knowledge, it merely allows arbitrary things to happen in the spaces which have not been controlled. The human environment is powerful, it affects all who breathe it in consistently. It affects the residents far more than those who travel in for daily contact and if both the staff and children are resident it will affect them both with equal vigour, even if not always in the same way. The human environment can be packaged into compartments for different types of community members and this not only establishes the 'us and them' environmental component, it also creates barriers, preventing one group from understanding what is happening to the other. Thus abuse can occur and continue to occur because the child believes that at worst all the staff are involved in the action, at least that they will condone it or protect each other.

All children face the same developmental tasks regardless of the institution in which they live. They need to grow into healthy and well-adjusted adults, developing a range of intellectual, social and occupational skills, relevant to their needs and circumstances. The positive human environment relates to the quality of experience offered to the child. It is inherent in the degree of opportunity available and the level of personal integrity and individual respect

accorded its members. It contains many elements of self determination and requires an availability of space into which the child can
grow. The negative human environment involves disempowerment,
vulnerability, ignorance and prejudice. It contains elements of
system dominance, inflexibility, disinvolvement and dehuman-
isation. Positive human environments allow children to develop
their own potential. Negative human environments repress all and
hold all but the powerful few in subservience.

It is not the case that there are some children with problems
and some children without problems. The concept of a problem
life situation is purely relative, and the impact of environmental
factors will vary from child to child, and, adult to adult. A boy
who is unhappy, feeling lonely and unaccepted will feel the pain
whether he is in a secure unit or a boarding school, a hospital ward
or a foster home. Staff can tell the child that there are children in a
worse plight, or that things will be better with time, but one cannot
expect that pain and anguish will vanish as a consequence of the
pragmatic truth which such propositions contain. All that can be
done is to attempt to reduce the impact of the stressors contributing
to that emotional state, achieving the minimal possible negative
impact for the child whilst introducing elements of the current
environment which are pleasurable, supportive and stimulating.
This may not resolve the pain, but it may help the child to cope
with the grief and pain. All that can be done is to decelerate
the negative impact of the emotional, psychological and physical
environment, and, if an actual deceleration cannot be achieved
then attempts should at least be made to prevent the child's pain
and anxiety accelerating further. This approach offers a realistic
way of controlling the human environment, seeking not to impose
a system upon the child but rather enabling the child to cope with
very real feelings. Learning how to cope with negative feelings is
an important developmental step for any child to face. Within
the virtual closed establishments, the promotion of a positive
human environment is the first requisite if such tasks are to be
met successfully.

The physical impact

The level of facilities available to an establishment will to a large
extent be dependent upon its size. Large institutions may have
sports-field, gymnasiums, play areas, a range of transport and

specialist equipment. Remove the impact of the facilities which large establishments can maintain however, and the argument in favour of large establishments begins to dwindle rapidly. In all aspects of residential provision there has been a move towards smaller groupings although often this has been achieved by breaking up the larger group into a number of smaller units. Such efforts have been fired by attempts to create higher levels of interpersonal involvement and more significant interrelationship structures amongst members. Undoubtedly the overall institutional managers have retained control, and the degree to which that control is obvious or enforced is recognised as having a significant effect upon the nature of the climate within the unit. Managers in such a situation face the almost unresolvable conflict of interest that lies in attempting to maintain managerial control over the group of staff working in the unit, whilst encouraging a degree of autonomy amongst the staff and children within that group or unit. It is difficult to know where the senior staff in an institution fit into the area of contact with the children. Moos (1974) suggests that the presence of senior staff within the unit can inhibit the behaviour of the staff working with clients. In situations where two staff work together there is a possibility that the presence of one may negatively affect the other. The interaction of various staffing dimensions has great relevance and importance in determining the quality of service offered within the unit. Age, sex, qualification, length of service, tenure of posts, and allocation of living quarters, all have a significance which does not go unnoticed within the establishment. Children gain their insight about the condition of the establishment through their perception of the actions and responses of staff. The degree of genuineness and support apparent in the staff actions will affect the child's belief in the value of the placement and its value to themselves.

Canter and Canter (1979) studied institutions for handicapped children and concluded that in the larger institutions staff were more institution orientated, whilst staff in smaller units were more child orientated. This may well be replicated across the range of residential provision.

The physical location of the establishment can serve to inhibit or promote the interaction of the resident with the local community. The location of the establishment may be considered a reflection of society's attitude towards that group. If the children in the establishment are deemed capable of involvement in the community then the establishment may be located openly in the community. This carries painful perceptions of reality for those who find themselves 'out in the wilds', or surrounded by physical barriers emphasising separation. Institutionalisation can be as much a result of socially constructed barriers as institutional practices, although there are probably more independent boarding schools 'out in the wilds' than there are residential care establishments. Is this an indication of the historical rejection of such schools or does it indicate that the establishments desire to be out of sight of the populace?

Internal features

The internal design of the establishment can incorporate a range of climatic enhancing features. Establishments with large rooms, high ceilings, drab decor, identical from room to room, displaying austere but functional furniture, produce an entirely different climate to that in establishments which have small, individually and warmly decorated rooms, each with their character determined by the choice of furnishings and decor. Arrangements for enabling and encouraging the children to personalise their own living areas, the extent to which they can attain privacy, the opportunities they are afforded to express their individuality and the extent to which they are encouraged to tolerate the individuality of others are vital determinants in the way in which children perceive the institutional climate. There are many clues given to the children about the relationship between themselves and the establishment. How often are the children permitted to use rooms and facilities for purposes other than those for which they were originally designed? How many rooms are organised for the benefit of the children. One establishment may retain a room for a single function, even though as such the room may be used for only two hours each Saturday and Sunday afternoon. Another establishment may use the room for a range of functions suggested by the residents themselves.

Seating arrangements within rooms play an important part in the operation of the care environment. Sociofugal arrangements actively discourage relationships and communication between the residents and yet they are often seen in residential establishments. Seats arranged around the wall, symmetrical furniture arrangements, seats in rows to facilitate easy group TV viewing, wide open spaces of carpet creating the feeling of crossing the parade ground for residents, seats in circles to facilitate meetings and sessions all serve to depersonalise the environment. Sociopetal arrangements however, actively encourage relationships, multi-person interaction and both private and personal communications and discussions. Furniture may be rearranged to provide a little privacy or even a little intimacy. Chairs in small groups permit discussions in which the individual may address a small, relaxed and chosen group, rather than having to perform before all staff and residents present in the room. Perhaps it is this very aspect which ensures that some staff seek to adopt sociofugal arrangements out of a mistrust of what it is that residents wish to discuss in private (or plot in secrecy).

There is a need for managers to take a careful look at the way in which residents are using the facilities offered within their establishment. Behaviour mapping is a technique in which the methods of counting heads and recording activities are used to record, on a time basis, who is doing what and where. Such information can provide insight into the use of the establishment and provide a basis for the structuring of facilities to meet resident need rather than staff perceptions of resident need which are inevitably based upon the staff's own frames of reference.

The internal design of the establishment and the degree to which physical situations are used to emphasise personal or social differences are important dimensions in determining climate. Staff may feel that it is necessary to have facilities away from the children. They may require situations which offer them security for their personal possessions, not allowing children into the 'staff areas', and requiring separate toilet and domestic facilities. All such situations influence the way in which children perceive the context of their own living situation and their place in the order of things.

Moos (1974) considered 'behaviour settings', an aspect of climate which has been researched mainly by Barker (1968). Behaviour settings have a significant impact upon the behaviour of those who live within them (Davison, 1990: 37). Certain types of environments demand certain types of behaviour. Students in small schools were seen by Barker as having fewer associates, but as experiencing twice the pressure to become involved in group activities. They were described as having to accept more areas of responsibility, being more likely to be challenged and to feel challenged, and more likely to gain cultural and moral values, than students in larger schools.

The dimensions of organisational structure were examined by Moos through the work of Porter and Lawler (1965) who had concluded that many organisational dimensions were significantly related to the attitudes or behaviours of the members. Moos looked at the way in which the personal characteristics of individuals in an institution, including age, ability, socio-economic background, and educational attainments affected the creation of a behavioural climate. The nature of the staff – child relationship is central to this. Staff practice often includes the collation of all relevant information about the child with the expressed purpose of enabling the staff to respond in a supportive and understanding manner. Are questions asked about the appropriateness of any individual member of staff's personal make-up, mental state or physical condition as being suitable for the task of meeting the needs of the children or handling such information? It is interesting to contemplate upon the sidedness of such arrangements. One may wonder how many staff would remain in their post if doing so was dependent upon them surviving the same intensely personal and deep-rooted investigative process as that experienced by the child during an assessment period.

Measuring environments

Moos (1974) initiated research in various settings including classrooms, which led to the development of instruments designed to measure climate in various settings. These instruments basically establish three dimensions, although a fourth, that of 'innovation' or 'change' is at times introduced. The first of these dimensions is the 'relationship dimension', which deals with the degree of involvement an individual has with the environment and the extent to which individuals support and help one another. The second of these dimensions is the 'personal development' dimension and this deals with the basic direction along which growth and self enhancement tends to occur in the particular environment. This dimension varies according to the nature of the institution under consideration. It also deals with the degree of autonomy extant, looking at the degree to which members are actually encouraged to be self sufficient and independent. The third dimension, 'system maintenance and system change', looks at the basic aspects of order and organisation, clarity of expectation, and staff control. The scales developed by Moos are valuable in that they offer an insight into the way in which elements of the environment can be conceptualised and analysed.

Applying the insight

In residential child care and education the quality of human relationships is central to the way in which the child perceives and values the human environment. The degree of involvement offered to children, the way in which children feel that they are an integral part of the community and are being accorded individual rights within that community are extremely important issues, closely linked to the way in which members of staff perceive their own role in relation to the behaviour presented by the children. These perceptions, and a good many others, contribute towards the quality and experience of institutional climate. Staff as leaders create different environments, sometimes offering a form of leadership upon which children will later model themselves. In the absence of parents, the staff provide the standards by which children learn to value themselves, developing the attitudes which will affect so much of their later thinking.

The impact of affiliation

The degree of affiliation felt by children will depend upon the extent to which children are able to feel that they are part of the group. It will determine how they are able to cope with feelings of being liked or disliked by others and in turn liking or disliking others, and the way in which they perceive friendship as an important aspect of the day-to-day intra-establishment functioning. This is an important area of interaction, shaping, as it does, the children's emotional and psychological understanding of both the place in which they live and their own place within it.

Feelings of affiliation are not purely the domain of the children. Members of staff within the establishment are as vulnerable to the effects of climate as any resident. The feelings of affiliation to the establishment are as pertinent for staff as those felt by the residents. Organisations may have inbuilt systems which create a 'contracting in' or a 'contracting out' response amongst its members. Members of staff who perceive that they are lacking an operable sense of affiliation with team mates or colleagues are at liberty to leave the establishment or even to relocate themselves elsewhere within the organisation. Children also encounter deep feelings of non-affiliation but they cannot respond as freely as the staff. In order to leave the organisation the child may well be forced into playing the role of an institutional offender. Children who attempt to adjust their position within the organisation are in danger of being seen as either anti-authority or anti-peer group. In most situations relocation is outside the child's sphere of control unless they deliberately raise the tariff level by indulging in persistent behaviour of a type designed to force others to remove him to another establishment on the basis that it may be more able to cope with such behaviour. There are huge dangers involved in children's attempts at relocating self. The 'Measurement of Treatment Potential' (MTP) is an interesting concept which was used in Canadian schools and centres for juvenile delinquents to assess this particular dimension of climate. Children are seen as reacting to their joint perception of the establishment by favouring the peers whose behaviour reflects that perception. If the residents choose other residents whose behaviour gains the approval of staff members then the MTP is deemed to be high. If the residents choose other residents whose behaviour emphasises the mismatch between staff and children's perceptions of a good selection, the MTP is said to be low.

Forming purposeful relationships

The child who can select his or her own companions, and is accepted by them without regard to artificial or organisational barriers, and the child who can maintain friendships made in the community prior to admission, will experience a higher degree of affiliation than the child who only meets prescribed people. Supporting others is often viewed as the golden mark of caring people, and many people have a picture of the residential worker as an overworked but caring person, warm and patient, loving and committed. Others have a different view. Sadly the impact of those who abuse their responsibilities attract a level of media coverage which those staff who conscientiously and purposefully meet their responsibilities can never achieve.

The staff who are charged with the domiciliary care and personal development of children are involved in the most fundamental process in the human life. There is no room for inattentiveness or laziness, the task is a 24 hour, seven day per week task. The success connected with the work is stupendous but the consequences of failure are awesome. More than in any other situation they have to commence duty by putting their own families, crises, personal expectations, hopes and aspirations to one side. Whether or not they are able to submerge such feelings, they will always communicate to children for whom they care, through a range of media, the true nature of the relationships they either enjoy or endure. Children in residential care often have difficulty in coping with staff who are suffering pain in their own lives. The children can all too easily see the adult's disturbance and it stimulates like feelings about their own lives. Empathy is an important tool for residential staff, but the children need whole, stable people to guide and assist them.

Children have their own developmental and personal problems. As they take on these struggles, they are persistently and consistently faced with the climatic consequences of their struggles. The institution is a poor battle ground for children exercising self defence when it is the institutional system against which they are defending themselves.

At the simplest level, many things which are of great importance to the child are affected by, and possibly dependent upon, the frame of mind with which the staff approaches the duty session. If staff are tired through decorating their home prior to duty, or through lack of sleep due to late night study, parties or the arrival of a new and inconsiderate member of the family, the way in which they perform in the residential setting with the children will be affected. The distractions are infinite. Awaiting delivery of a new car, news of interview outcomes or results of examinations will cause staff to be distracted. If staff are disillusioned with the establishment, lacking a feeling of affiliation or involved in conflicts with the system, members of their line management team or colleagues, they will be unable to function normally in meeting their caring and enabling role. It is impossible for members of staff to attend successfully to the needs of their establishment children if they are only presenting themselves in part, switching out their personal life, operating only the minimal skills and personality aspects which the organisation requires.

Each member of staff is as complex and unique as the individual children for whom they care. Given a fluctuating level of performance based upon personal circumstances, staff will respond arbitrarily in a range of situations important to the child. Members of staff must maintain a high level of sensitivity to the children's needs and circumstances so that they can respond appropriately to the child. Staff must be able to empathise with the children's situation, ensuring that the children's problems are understood and attended to with sincerity and urgency, that their parents and friends are afforded respect and friendliness, and that their confidences are handled appropriately and delicately. At all times the children must see that consideration is given to their feelings, attitudes, points of view and wishes. When they perceive such things in adult responses towards them, they are offered far clearer indications of the true nature of the child – staff relationship than promises, voiced intentions, assurances and explanations could ever offer. Where staff and children share rights and responsibilities a positive human environment will result.

Given the central importance of staff to aspects of establishment functioning, it is essential that any attempt to define and understand the climate of an establishment should include an attempt to analyse the stress factors experienced by staff. Managers need to know when staff are under pressure, and the extent to which that member of staff can cope with the stress in an efficient, healthy and mangeable way. The managers should be aware of the ways in which members of staff defend themselves from the effects of stress, and the ways in which such defending affects the climate of the establishment (Davison, 1985).

Enabling personal growth

Elements of the personal-growth dimension can be usefully applied by an understanding of the nature of residential work in the context of climate. Competition has its place in society, but the damage suffered by some children through having to compete must be clearly recognised. Despite the universal acceptance that unchecked competition can be damaging, children in residential and educational group settings are thrown into, potentially, the greatest competitive arena of all, that of competition for primary affection and attention. Staff must find some way of meeting the individual needs of large groups of children, each of whom manifests in different ways, a fundamental need for attention. It is inevitable that in such situations, competition will be perceived by the child as a consequence of the presence of other children who are desperate to receive attention from the same members of staff, whether staff have consciously contributed towards that competition or not. It is extremely tempting for staff to use the granting of such attention as a control response and thus create the situations by which the child who is most successful in meeting staff expectations is the child who will continue to be successful in receiving staff attention. All children (and adults) need attention albeit to varying degrees. The children who do not seek attention are not children who do not need attention, they are more likely to have accepted that there is little chance of achieving the attention they wish to receive from adults. They may have already switched attention-seeking behaviour away from primary adults either towards members of their peer group, or less well-intentioned adults. All children benefit from attention and involvement with interested and friendly adults during the course of their personal development. If children cannot achieve such involvement through normal routes, they may become vulnerable to obtaining it through less acceptable routes. A young girl or boy, feeling unloved within the family can be moved to promiscuous sex, giving sex for attention, thus gaining a physical alternative to the emotional warmth he or she desires. Why should this not also be true of a child in the residential group care or boarding school setting, especially in large institutions where there is a significantly reduced opportunity for involvement with adults. Homosexual activities between boys in such settings cannot be entirely the consequence of childish curiosity. Not all abused children recognise that they are being abused. The child is an amazingly adaptable organism which needs cues as to the direction in which development should take place.

The staff – child divide

The staff – child interaction offers many cues to the child. The extent to which a child's expressed feelings can become a basis for the rethinking of decisions by staff; the degree to which a child is permitted to have personal feelings about the establishment functioning and the extent to which those feelings can be expressed; the extent to which the child can express dissatisfaction about the behaviour of others, including staff – are all factors which determine the climatic potential for personal growth in the establishment. Such factors are not only controlled largely by staff in respect of the children, but are also applicable to the staff themselves. Their exalted position of power in no way removes the influences and impact of the multidimensional climate upon them. It is also relevant to consider the way in which staff are able to express feelings about the establishment and the degree of encouragement offered by the management team to do so. As with children, staff perceptions play an important role in this process. Staff who feel personally threatened by such expressions of disagreement will tend to over-react, over-control and over-punish children who fail to follow the accepted line. Alternatively, staff who have genuine insight into the child's developmental needs may well feel the need to listen to the child and discuss the point openly and reflectively. Moos (1974) observes that qualified staff tend to concentrate on the importance of the personal growth dimension, feeling that the dimensions of system maintenance were more likely to get in the way of the real task of treatment. Interestingly for managers engaged in the 'are qualifications necessary?' debate, this treatment orientation was reversed amongst non-qualified staff who placed more emphasis on systems maintenance than personal-growth dimensions. However, the research stressed that there appeared to be little significant difference in the quality of the relationships which existed between each group of staff and their patients. This raises fundamental questions as to the relationship between the treatment aims and methods, and the reasons why the application of rules and regulations interfere with the provision of treatment.

Staff control is a positive factor in the maintenance of working relationships within the establishment. There is a clear need for staff to establish boundaries in a clear and enabling manner. Indeed Moos suggests, 'some programs with active treatment milieus encouraging the open expression of anger may make patients more uncomfortable, thereby causing a decrease in helping behaviour'.

Supporting the system

Many of Moos' systems-maintenance subscale factors have obvious implications for the residential group care setting. The traditionally high degree of institutional organisation required to facilitate neatness and cleanliness amongst residents has been a significant factor in residential care observed as long ago as in the Curtis Report of 1946 in which the military precision of sleeping arrangements and the regimentation of normal life experiences were condemned. Undoubtedly there is a constant source of conflict in establishments where the pressure to maintain the children in a clean and presentable state is not always welcomed by all children. Staff must ensure that children are well dressed, clean in habits and presentation, well fed, and living in standards of good physical condition, but to ensure that this happens in batch living situations it is necessary to institute rotas and timetables. This is a fundamental, climate-determining dimension and it is of great value to ascertain its basis. Where in the establishment are decisions about the nature of the child's normal life experiences made? Who decides time happenings? Who decides what the children wear, what they eat, what they plan to eat, whether or not they should be able to make themselves a snack or a drink, visit the local shops or cinema, go to work or school, have a bath, a haircut or hairdo, spend money or save money, go on a diet, take up a sport, become involved with a boyfriend or girlfriend? Are the children allowed to decide the arrangements of furniture in their own bedrooms? What arrangements are made for smokers? Are special areas provided for those who are allowed to smoke?; who decides which brand of cigarettes they smoke, who holds the cigarettes and who controls their use? What arrangements are available to decide whether or not the child should go home for a weekend, that the child is too ill to go to school, or, should or can get a part-time job? Can children have pets, can they play records and cassettes, switch on TV, have visitors, or choose to sleep in late?

Discussions of the effects of establishment size upon climate, indicate that the larger the establishment, the greater the opportunity for child-centred practices to be squeezed out often in favour of establishment-centred practices. Moos (1974) observes,

> Large size may create organizational pressures toward custodial rather than treatment operations. The custodial atmosphere may itself create 'unreceptive' behaviour, which justifies the need for further regimentation. Thus large size may initiate staff behaviours, especially staff control.

The effectiveness of establishment rules and regulations are dependent upon the clarity with which those rules are expressed. Clearly defined rules leave little room for misunderstanding and children know exactly where they stand and what will happen if they transgress the rules. They know what is punishable and what is not. Often they know what form the punishment will take, who will administer it and whether or not they feel it is fair. Lack of rule clarity can lead to uncertainty and the manipulation of the staff by children, and this can lead to an inconsistent application of the rules by different staff with different children. Rule clarity can have its drawbacks. Clearly defined rules and regulations can create inflexibility and remove the potential for staff to use discretion in meeting children's individual needs by ensuring a uniform and strict adherence to the rules and regulations.

Coping with change

Change which is imposed upon an establishment has many different operational effects to those which are generated internally. The decision makers are always the most committed to supporting change and this is equally true where children initiate or participate in the decisions which bring changes to both their own living situations and their own lives. Staff who feel committed to a small unit within a larger establishment may feel frustration and disenchantment with changes which are seen as being imposed from elsewhere in the establishment. This perception is affected by the nature of the institution's philosophy. Some establishments may have a single agreed philosophy which underwrites the daily work of the establishment, others may have mixed and competing ideologies. The philosophy of an establishment can easily get lost in the day-to-day tasks of residential living. Philosophic differences can be the source of great conflict between staff, especially where separate house-unit managers are accorded a great deal of autonomy. In some residential establishments, the teaching staff and the house-parents adopt entrenched positions. By doing so they severely restrict the establishment's ability to incorporate change in a healthy and meaningful way. Staff attitudes are a major influence in residential group living settings and marked differences in staff attitudes can create observable different climatic effects. Restrictive control as opposed to protective care not only impacts upon the facility to change, but also has a substantial effect upon the nature of the relationships developed. Warmth and a willingness to discuss problems may be associated with over permissiveness, whereas authoritarianism can be associated with inflexibility and defensive protectionism.

The degree to which staff conform to each other's views or more importantly to the primary themes of establishment philosophy, has a substantial impact upon the establishment's ability to control change mechanisms. Certain processes serve to maintain a high degree of conformity amongst staff's expressed attitudes and response patterns thus enabling the maintenance of a stable environmental climate. Continuous contact with a group of like-thinking colleagues can have a powerful effect upon the development of attitudes in a participating individual, often resulting in group conformity. The strength of these self-selection processes can serve to diminish the real effect of change within an establishment. Change occurring in establishments often implies the removal or alteration of institutional practices and responses which are the basis of many senior staff members claims to seniority. This carries the implication that for some members of senior staff, change is a threat to status, especially if they are not actually involved in initiating, implementing or influencing the direction in which change is moving. If this is the case, then it is not unreasonable to expect that opposition to change from this quarter will be a potent and somewhat incestuous force. Change may be seen as a threat to personal validity rather than a positive institutional development. As the empowering of children poses a threat to some staff, so the enabling of junior staff can threaten senior staff. Institutional change involves a large element of risk as existing practices are broken down and new ones developed, and as such it is a potential source of trouble and conflict. Often innovations have to be successful before they are implemented, thus minimising the risk of failure for the manager. The number of institutional barriers which can be encountered by an individual intent on initiating change does not reduce the intrinsic value of the change, even though it may reveal problems which have been previously hidden. Change must occur. The whole process of residential group care and education has for many years been based upon the premiss that change of some nature will occur and that hopefully it will occur in a positive and enabling form. Some commentators link the progress of residential care to the process of catastrophic change, believing that improvements can only follow disasters.

The house the Act built

Although the physical facilities of the establishment remain relatively fixed within the physical framework of the establishment, much can be achieved within that framework (see Volume 5, 3.4.1, and Volume 4, 1.58, 1.71). Colours, textures and the quality of materials used in furnishings and furniture make a significant contribution to improving the quality of life. Displaying children's pictures, drawings and models will prove far more beneficial to the child's sense of involvement than the neatest bulletin board displaying timetables, rotas, official communications and Fire Department regulations. Personal items in institutional settings can serve to enhance the child's feelings of affiliation. Flowers and plants in pots, ornaments and photographs can assist to foster a sense of belonging.

The phrase 'purpose built' is often used, however, one is forced to ask, 'For whose purpose, and, for what purpose was it (really) built?' Attractive garden layouts may create great practical problems for staff dealing with disturbed, deprived and difficult children, many of whom will see little reason to stick to paths but rather pursue a direct-line policy in even the most inclement weather. Positive independent elements of design and building can come together to create very negative experiences for residents and staff. Such 'purpose-built' establishments often give the visitor a tremendous insight into the ingenuity of staff in creating antidotes to environmental constraints.

The appointment of the heads of establishments provides the leadership element. It is the single most important element in climatic variable determination. The Utting Report (1991: 13) emphasises the importance of the head of the establishment as 'the biggest single influence'. Yet too often, appointments are based upon the perceived individual qualities of the candidate rather than the commitment to, or experience of, the desired establishment functioning pattern. The best man is not always the best man for the job. To appoint staff regardless of their ability to contribute to the existing climate is to create potential for conflict. To appoint staff widely without such regard will undoubtedly result in a functional breakdown in the establishment. As a new head takes up a post, the degree to which he is in agreement with the existing climate of the establishment will determine the degree to which he will initially be in conflict with his new staff. The interplay of relationships, personal development needs and system-maintenance dimensions are elements of the environment in which conflict is often experienced by the staff and imposed upon the residents. The person appointed should be the best person to continue the good work of the establishment, maintaining the status quo whilst initiating change.

In search of a discipline

The study of the climatic elements in an establishment can lead to the realisation that despite the undoubted importance and fundamental influence of climate, climate as a concept remains elusive. In attempting to describe the climatic factors contributing to the experience that is climate, it is by necessity incumbent upon the researcher to consider all aspects of the establishment functioning, especially those areas or elements which are normally seen as being mundane, fixed and unthinkingly accepted within the establishment. If climate is an experience of environment which determines the nature of the environment then it is by definition all pervading. It is as relevant in the quiet daily grind of domestic routines as it is in the turbulence and passion of crisis management. It is as apparent in the physical structures as in the attitudes of staff and the operations of the organisational system.

Whilst residential group care is weary of the high degree of scrutiny to which it has been subjected during the last decade, boarding education is experiencing its first shock waves. Despite the reduction in the residential bed provision, there is a growing acceptance that for some children the option of living in residential care is a realistic and valued option. A similar pattern has been seen to apply in the independent boarding school sector where many schools are seriously addressing the problems of a decreased residential demand. Although it is appropriate that children should be received into residential care when no acceptable and natural alternative exists, it is strongly argued that for some children there will always be the need for the residential provision that is an alternative nurturing system to that offered by the family. There will always be children for whom natural family life has ended and substitute family life is an intolerable burden with which they are unable to cope. There will always be children who wish or need to be educated away from home, or who are unable to live with their parents in the normal way. In all establishments, regardless of status or function, there is a need to ensure that the whole needs of the child are met. The institution must do so with a high degree of insight and knowledge of its own capabilities, potential, effectiveness and inadequacies, and a sound understanding of the child's personal and developmental needs. Concurrently, every possible precaution must be taken to ensure that hurt, damage or deprivation are not inflicted unwittingly upon the child.

The study of climate offers great scope to those involved in designing or managing residential, educational and group care settings. One day the study of residential climate will come to be valued as a professional discipline in its own right, but until then managers will be left to pull together whatever is available. Managers must constantly search for new resources. The greatest environmental influence and resource available are the staff who work within the establishment and it is this influence and resource which must be enabled, 'there is no limit to what the average person can accomplish if thoroughly involved' (Peters, 1987: 282).

Investing in the future: the staffing dimension

Perhaps the most crucial aspect of the residential experience lies in the human relationships. Staff influence and shape climate, they design, interpret and operate the organisational processes and administrative tasks that contribute towards climate. They provide the contact which largely determines the emotional climate, and they carry the attitudes, hopes and aspirations which will influence the motivational climate. Significantly, although the staff are in many ways deeply involved in the shaping of climatic determinants, they themselves are equally as vulnerable to the effects of the climate as any resident. They too are directed by it, affected by it and shaped by it and thus any attempt to define the climate of an establishment should, after the physical analysis, be a study of the staff. The 1989 Children Act offers an opportunity to provide for the future of children who live away from home. There is a need to invest in the physical environment and a need to research all elements of institutional climate. Most of all there is a need to invest in the staff, implementing valid recruitment, training and retention programmes. Residential care and boarding staff must together form a professional base, equivalent to the European social pedagogue or social educator, with appropriate training and qualification programmes. It is essential that those who manage the residential managers are residential staff themselves. For too long the adults who care for other people's children have been marginalised and minimalised. They have failed to share their knowledge and skills, or to demand that they be afforded the professional development and status which the responsibilities of their work demand. The Utting Report (1991: 17) addresses this situation directly. Section 86 relates to the need to accord appropriate status to carers as well as appropriate payment, conditions of service and training. Section 87 addresses the reality of the task facing carers. Section 88 stresses the need to not only make significant improvements in the service now, but also to co-ordinate the residential strategy, ensuring that caring becomes a valued occupation.

It is a national scandal that it has been necessary to set up a special programme to ensure that all heads of children's homes can obtain at least a basic qualification within the next five years. Would this situation have been tolerated in schools or hospitals? What then of the staff employed in children's homes? Often independent boarding schools treat the care provision as secondary to the real task of education, rarely even bothering to provide separate staff let alone appropriately qualified staff. In some boarding schools the task of caring for children is a penance the housemaster must pay in order to gain the credentials necessary to become an applicant headmaster. The application of the available child-care knowledge base gained in hospital wards, children's homes, residential special schools and other institutions which have to care for children whilst carrying out other essential tasks, is at best patchy. There are some specialist units and therapeutic establishments which have been far more successful in tackling this task, but in many others little has been achieved. The answer lies in the hands of the range of the staff who work in the most human of environments, residential care.

The psychological environment is shaped by each human, emotional, physical and organisational interaction which occurs in the group care establishment. The buildings, the children, the organisation and the staff are all component parts and all can be used and enabled, restricted and denied by the psychological environment they conspire to create. Ignorance of these factors and the way they interact gives permission for the unnecessary, the unacceptable and the inhuman. If the establishment is to positively and appropriately meet the needs of both staff and children it must control, guide and nurture each of the elements, maintaining a positive control over the whole structure. If it does not, the psychological environment will, without plan or reason, control and direct all who live within its power. Managing establishments is ultimately about managing the psychological environment for the benefit of those who live, work and grow within it.

CHAPTER 9

Is it Safe to Touch?

Norman M. Cooke

Introduction

The physical and sexual abuse of children has been an increasing
cause of concern in recent times. Suggestions that the problem may
have been present for a long time, that it is not merely a recent
cause for alarm, are unhelpful. The need to address what may be
happening, and to prevent it occurring now and in the future, is
all important.

These two forms of abuse, physical and sexual, fall well
beyond the parameters of behaviours to which many in society
are accustomed or indeed would find acceptable. In retrospect it
would appear that some incidents have gone unreported. Whilst
speculation attempts to reason for the lack of reporting in the
past, we can be sure of one thing, attitudes alter over time. For
sexual abuse to be the topic of conversation, or warrant coverage
by the media, 15 or 20 years ago, would have been unthinkable
and whilst incest, or 'taking advantage' of minors would have been
reported, there would have been no use of the word 'abuse' in such
reports.

By labelling this practice as 'abuse', the full revulsion of
what is happening is rightly brought to mind. Hence, 'sexual
abuse', 'physical abuse', and even more recently 'satanic abuse'
immediately conjure up a picture of something completely
unacceptable, and of which most individuals would find
repulsive.

These forms of abuse are not confined to family homes, but
are now reported to have occurred in the different types of
establishment where children are found. This includes residential
educational establishments. Whilst legislation (such as the Children
Act) and better management practice, attempt to ensure such
incidents do not occur in the future, a void appears to have

opened up in response to fear of professional behaviours being subsequently interpreted as abuse.

Physical and sexual abuse involves touching. Indeed, apart from the accompanying emotional abuse, the majority of physical and sexual abuse must involve touching. The writer is concerned that carers, whether in the classroom, bedroom or dormitory, or whatever environment that is currently occupied by a child have become frightened to come into contact with those for whom they care in case the motives behind that touching is misconstrued. As a result of this, touching may become taboo. Physical contact is discouraged. There are no rules or guidelines governing this. In fact, no-one really addresses the issue. This is very sad. The neglect of positive touching can only be to the detriment of a child. In order to be safe, many adults adopt the attitude of 'hands off'. It is insufficient to adopt this attitude, for the positive aspects of touch are also lost when touching is abandoned.

There is literature relating to the subject of 'touch', but it lies beyond the field of education. The following test offers a number of ideas which have been brought together as a result of experiences of working in and visiting various residential establishments. The most recent experiences relate to working in a hospital school which provides education for adolescents in a psychiatric hospital, with both secure and open facilities. In order to develop the ideas further it is necessary to investigate the child's point of view on the subject. Indeed, to be in keeping with the Children Act, this is paramount. The following discussion is adult orientated in order to generate an appropriate discussion of the subject.

There may be some expectation that residential educational establishments should to some extent reflect what would otherwise happen if the boarder lived at home. This may sound rather a nonsense. If the need has arisen for a child to go somewhere other than an educational establishment local to their home, why should it follow that this alternative setting should in any way reflect what may have happened at home? Some may argue that a homely environment is irrelevant when considering educational needs, that the education of the individual has nothing to do with home comforts. Whilst teachers may act *in loco parentis* this does not necessarily mean that they have to take on all the different roles of a parent. They have the same responsibilities as a parent, but they are not obliged or encouraged to enter into the role of a substitute parent.

Furthermore, the age of the boarder may necessitate entirely different needs. The sixth-form boarder should be better equipped to meet the world away from home, than an eleven year old, or even younger. The teacher/carer needs to respond according to the age and need of those who are within their care.

Establishments which provide residential education may not necessarily consciously promote a homely environment (specifically the built environment) or a group of carers who attempt to mirror mother, father or sibling relationships. Yet within such provision there are usually those who have evolved, to some extent, elements of these roles. With some irony perhaps, it is frequently the case that those who are adopted as surrogate parents are not always those whom the system identifies as appropriate. In many residential establishments it is not the headmaster nor senior management team whom the pupil turns to in time of need. It is not the subject teacher. It is not always the housemaster/mistress whom they turn to. There is further irony here, in that these, of all people, are those whom the establishment may well recognise as the first person to whom the child should turn if a crisis appears to be looming. It may be the domestic help or matron who not only know what is happening but also are the ones in whom the pupils confide when they need to do so. The child may find it difficult to discuss what may be a trivial problem or a major catastrophe with 'teachers'. Aspects of confidentiality immediately come into play. There is a problem in confiding in the headmaster, subject teacher or housemaster, and not expecting them to act upon the information imparted. Advice may be appropriate sometimes, but many problems will need to be shared with others in order to seek a solution. Some will involve contact with home, with parents and siblings. Others will involve less formal relationships, for example the domestic help or matron who are seen as not being restricted by having to act on the information presented, and as such they act as a sounding board. At times individuals need someone with whom to share problems or moans, someone to ask about relationships with peers or staff, someone with whom to share emotions.

Some residential establishments have carefully identified houseparents as opposed to housemasters/mistresses. There would seem to be some conflict in role between the teacher and the housemaster when they are one and the same person. If houseparents are desirable, if the matron or domestic assistants do provide a role beyond that for which they are employed, what is it that they can provide which the teacher/housemaster cannot?

All teachers act *in loco parentis* but what is it that makes a parent and which aspect of parenting are teachers supposed to replicate? Furthermore what is it that constitutes a family in this day and age, and what implications are there for trying to provide a 'family' atmosphere within the residential education setting?

Whilst the extended family gave way to the nuclear family in the 1960s we can now identify many varied different sub-cultures of the nuclear family. Social agencies continue to present the nuclear family as the 'norm' but there are many variations on the theme here. We now have the one-parent family, where one parent is separated from the other by death, divorce, desertion, separation or increasingly by choice. There are one-parent families where the child does not even know what it is to have a father. There are families where brothers and sisters may only share one common parent (that is, step-families). There are families where both parents work, and sometimes virtually from the time the child is born. There is no underlying inference of criticism in the different families identified above. The question to address is simply if a child is away from home requiring both education and accommodation, which family role model should be adopted? One may ask; is there a universal family role model available today? Should a surrogate mother and father figure be an integral feature of such schools, or is this unfair and unrealistic for those children who have never known such figures at home? Can anyone ever fulfil such a role anyway and if so what does it involve? In what way is it different to being a teacher?

There are many features in common between teachers and parents. Indeed many teachers are parents and to some extent have added advantages in this respect. There are differences however which require some closer inspection. Traditionally the home environment has provided adult role models during early childhood. These have normally been parent role models. This is increasingly not the case as many young children attend 'child minders' whilst both parents have become bread winners. The direct contact time between parent and child remains all the more important as distinct bonding between the two occurs here. The bonding here is amplified and secured by cuddling/embracing. The touching between parent and child right from this very early age is more than natural and desirable, it is crucial for the child's initial and later well-being. Through touch, the parent feeds, cleans, loves and protects the child. The child is carried at least until they can walk, and usually far beyond that as well.

One of the fundamental differences between specific (non-teaching) carers and teachers, is closely related to ideas about touch. Touch is an immensely powerful expression of emotion which can be used positively within relationships. Alternatively the most dreadful negative consequences come about when used in a manner perceived as abusive by the recipient. There is much reporting and documentation about negative touch which has been found in some residential environments. The appalling and disgusting incidents of physical and sexual abuse became regular newspaper reports in the 1980s. The Children Act 1989 attempts to address these issues in order to ensure that such incidents should not occur now or in the future. It is imperative that a system is present in all establishments which permits reporting of anything untoward, at the first opportunity. Some recently reported cases have only come to light, years after the abuse has taken place.

For a teacher to touch a pupil may be both undesirable and foolish. There are exceptions, but there is little if any documentation or guidelines as to what they are.

The parent – child touch changes over time. There are partly cultural reasons for this. For example, in Britain for a man to kiss a male baby or young boy may be acceptable if they are closely related. Few adult or teenage males openly kiss each other no matter how closely related they are. Likewise, an embrace is usually only encountered between adult or teenage males if they are closely related, or there is a very close friendship, and they have not met for some time. There are no hard and fast rules governing this. The normal response or most common responses would appear to be those outlined above, however, ideas on touch are culture bound. Here the interest is in what happens in British society.

There are two touch responses which are inappropriate. One could be described as assault (sexual or physical) the other relates to non-touching. It is anticipated that from an early age, children are guided by their parents/carers as to which areas of their body are inappropriate to touch. It is, therefore, of interest to consider how body touch cues are learned by the child. Generally, children learn from their families how to converse and communicate with each other. The intonation in utterances are not specifically taught, but children soon learn to identify the difference between 'no' and 'NO!' Likewise, much body language is also not overtly taught. Children almost know instinctively not to burst into conversation with someone who has their head lowered and is apparently crying.

These means of communication are established from an early age and are ongoing throughout our lives. We amend and shape them as our own personalities develop during adolescence and beyond. A quietly spoken individual can be both comforting and calming in a volatile situation. A wink or a finger to an eyebrow can become a greeting gesture. There are many variations on this theme. All are used by adults, adopted by those in their care and employed, modified or rejected by them.

Such utterances and body-language statements will be found in most societies. They are especially highlighted in all schools. The uniqueness and individuality of all pupils and staff could probably be described along these lines, just as much as their academic or sporting achievements.

As educators, we would be quick to challenge pupils whose intonations were sarcastic or put down those around them. We would also intervene if a pupil adopted a threatening stance with another. The utterance, the body language, is not acceptable. That which has been incorrectly identified as correct by the child, whether from an early age or later in its development, is thus challenged and alternative ideas are put forward for discussion and use by the individual concerned.

Sometimes conflict is brought about, even within the cues which have not been specifically taught, but rather acquired experimentally. Some inappropriate responses are also learned this way. Some adults scream and shout at children often belittling them, yet the children are encouraged not to respond in the same way. Some adults assume the authority necessary to justify their invasion of the child's personal space. A reciprocal arrangement is not allowed.

We speak, we hear, we look. From these three, a fairly comprehensive picture is built up of the environment around us. All manner of things happen and become part of the learning process from the moment we are born into this world. Whether we go on to live at home or reside away from home, our interactions with peers and adults sharpen up our means of communicating with each other, maintaining the learning process.

What about touch? The development features described above are all part of the hidden curriculum within schools. They happen and they are learned throughout school life. They would still happen even if there was no schooling, as they are ongoing as part of daily life anyway. The fact that they also occur in school gives some hope that appropriate strategies can be employed for dealing with them. Touch is quite different.

If consideration is given to the brief history of touching in schools, specifically between staff and pupils, it is doubtful that it would make good reading. Reference is made here to previous ideas relating to inappropriate touch. There are many examples of these, indeed they may be documented in some instances. Until the abolition of corporal punishment, the most likely chance of physical contact between pupil and teacher was at the end of a strap or cane. Incredible physical beatings are recorded until quite recently. Indeed, viewing the punishment book at governors' meetings was an integral part of school life until very recently. Some of these records make appalling reading, especially if they date back any length of time. The occurrence of gross incidents of sexual abuse have been mentioned earlier. It would appear that such incidents were more prevalent in residential settings than had been realised. Again until recently, some of these incidents were so serious and so degrading, that one can well believe the victim would not report such incidents for fear of not being believed, fear of even worse abuse, or shame or guilt at not recognising or reporting the abuse at an earlier stage.

At the other extreme to physical and sexual abuse as a form of touch, there is the deliberate act of not touching at all. Whilst this is without doubt the safest way for a teacher to behave, and leaves no doubt about what may be misinterpreted, it could also be argued that this is as demoralising as the physical or sexual abuse.

By considering a family model, any family, how important is touch to their everyday functioning? Consideration of this question should cause it to become apparent that touch is at least as important as other means of communication. Experience suggests that within the confines of a family there is naturally an amount of touching between parents, parent and child, and child and siblings. The child observes its parents embracing, cuddling, holding hands, and kissing each other. The parent can likewise embrace, cuddle, kiss and hold hands with the child. They can also physically hold their child back, preventing them from doing anything which they consider undesirable. They hold their child when the child has fallen. They share occasions of success and failure by embracing. A cuddle is a very powerful symbol of deep affection. When a child is hurt it communicates 'I'm sorry about what you're going through. Whilst I'm not at the exact point you are at now, I have been there and I have some understanding about what you're going through.' With success a cuddle can display the pleasure and pride associated with that success. A similar form of touching takes place between siblings. There is much more touching going on than this. A hand on the shoulder can speak far more than words alone. Play fighting, tickling, these are all safe within the parameters of a stable family. They can enhance respect for the integrity of each other and help to identify the boundaries as to what is acceptable behaviour and what is not.

Other forms of touch observed in the family involve the interaction of parents and the other adults about them. The simple hand shake is all too often overlooked and yet it can be a genuine greeting reinforcing the 'I am pleased to be with you.' The embrace and kiss, or the lack of both, helps the child to develop some means of identifying the difference between close friends and acquaintances within the adult peer group.

All the positive types of touch may be described as appropriate touch. They are initially learned within the family. Provided they are all appropriate, they create an important part of the child's development, at least as much as those other stimuli talked about earlier (talking, listening and looking). There is little inappropriate touch which happens within the home. That which does, ties in with what was described earlier, physical or sexual touch, or no touching at all. All three can leave the individual very isolated with a distorted perspective of life. If appropriate touch is a part of family life, can it ever be used within residential educational settings. Indeed is there any need for it?

One main concern must lie with pupils of primary age who board away from home. Adolescents, however, are really not all that far behind. Whilst adolescents needs may be different, they are no less important to the individual concerned.

Let us consider first the degree of touching which goes on with a boarder at present. Two forms come to mind immediately. There is the handshake when some award is presented (many may never achieve this) and there are contact games in sport. There are likely to be other incidental and social incidents of touch. Gender also comes into play here. Girls will often embrace arms when walking to lessons. They also tend to confide to each other in small groups huddled together, where there is considerable physical contact. Whilst these are all acceptable, are they sufficient? There is also bullying and fighting (play and otherwise). These are definitely not positive ideas about touch. The unfortunate things is (and that really is putting it mildly) that many can go for weeks, or terms without any experience of appropriate touch. When it is viewed in cold black and white it seems quite incredible that such a situation as this can arise. Is it possible for teachers to adopt any of the appropriate forms of touch as practised within families? Furthermore, is it at all desirable and are there any guidelines to consider?

Touch can be a useful indicator about a person. To touch a child on their elbow, when circumstances permit, can give some indication as to their previous encounters with touching. There is no suggestion of sweeping statements here, it can only act as a further indicator. If there is no response to the touching, it may suggest the child is used to being touched and is currently agreeable to it. Alternatively, a child who physically bristles and withdraws at the slightest touch would perhaps suggest some of those negative ideas of non-touch, or even the negative experience of physical or sexual abuse. There is also no suggestion that all should start touching everyone for evidence of abuse, this would be a further nonsense.

Experience recalls situations where touching has occurred and caused alarm to those involved. I recall some years ago finding two boys 'play fighting'. I had only been working at the CHE for a short time. I knew both boys by name, but little about them. The older and bigger boy was tormenting the younger one, who was apparently suffering as a consequence. I asked both boys to stop and calm down, which they did not do. I then tried to separate them, pulling them apart by holding their hands. The older boy physically bristled as I touched him. He froze and told me to back off. I recall the anger in his eyes. His play fighting changed to anger at me for touching him. I did back off, and said nothing more at the time. The situation calmed after a short time. Later enquiries revealed that this older boy had been sexually abused by another person. My touch, and all that I represented, an authoritive power requiring him to conform, was apparently interpreted as another dominant male forcing him against his will. This was a lesson hard learned by me, but one which made me much more aware of the implications of what touching may create.

An alternative touch is when the pupil touches the teacher. This is not to be confused with brushing past the teacher, but when the teacher is left in no doubt that a pupil has deliberately had a need to touch them. This is not an everyday occurrence either! Occasionally, pupils of either gender feel the need to have physical contact with another supportive person. There is a danger here of the other person handling the situation badly. Many forms of response or reaction could be displayed. It may be quite appropriate to infer or state quite strongly, 'Back off, that is not acceptable'. This involves no consideration of why the child had the need to touch in the first place. It may be assumed that the touch was to provoke flirting with the teacher concerned, but often children seek a physical environment of security offered by a parent, and the child may be searching for support in the absence of the usual or preferred source of support and security. The underlying concern by the person doing the touching could be a genuine cry for affection and not flirtation in nature. It may be a cry for help, the individual concerned unable to verbalise strong, emotional, troubled feelings. The perceived rejection of the child by the adult can be a further put-down to the pupil. Hence there is an inherent need to handle each situation delicately and on its own merits.

The pupil touching the teacher needs to experience a well-thought-out and positive response. This may still be a 'Back off' response, and as such it can remain a positive reaction by the teacher to the situation. It is important that the teacher considers all the reasons and possible responses, including their repercussions, to the situation which has arisen.

Amongst the children with whom I had worked was a girl who had been sexually abused. She was 16, and over a period of weeks took to the habit of putting her arms around me and embracing me in a cuddle. What she was doing was not appropriate because it prevented the maintenance of physical distance between us. She had many problems. The temptation for me was to chastise her for what she was doing. However, to do this would be another put down, another rejection. For whatever reason, she had found someone she felt 'comfortable' with. It was not as though we were ever alone − and that is immensely important. Neither did she have a 'crush' on me. What she did have, though perhaps did not realise it at the time, was a need for affection, from someone she could trust. Her way of expressing this was to embrace, or for want of a better word – cuddle!

Very occasionally the situation can arise when an embrace takes place between teacher and pupil. This is rare and requires very careful handling. There can be few circumstances when a teacher would openly initiate the embracing of a child. Bereavement may be one exception, as would the example of considerable trauma. The embrace is a very personal gesture. It exposes one's own personal space, a space which for many is usually kept very private. Only under these exceptional circumstances might it be employed.

For a pupil to embrace a teacher, is equally rare, but also requires the careful handling mentioned earlier. Again the age of the pupil is important here. The younger child may embrace in a moment of total forgetfulness – as when they inadvertently refer to the teacher as 'Mum' when this is an obvious mistake. When the adolescent initiates it, it is quite different. For the teacher to physically bristle and give the message 'Get off' could be the right message delivered in the wrong way, but once again there are alternative strategies to at least consider. Again an assessment needs to be given as to whether it is a flirtatious embrace, or a cry for genuine affection, or a need for reassurance by the child. The response from the teacher can have a profound effect upon the pupil's self esteem. To reject a genuine appeal is almost a form of abuse in itself. Surely the child has not grasped the acceptable nature of touch and needs careful counselling to explain the implications of their behaviour. This could be a tactful and appropriate response which can be made by the teacher. Where the embrace has been accepted there comes a point when disengagement must ensue. The prolonged embrace with no eye contact, no means of perceiving body language, and no conversation is most definitely not appropriate. The message given to the child will be false as there is a danger that this will be seen as an intimate, affectionate embrace. What needs to happen is for the adult to initiate at least a partial disengagement. The embrace needs to become a 'sideways cuddle'. That is, the adult places an arm across the child's shoulders at the back of the neck. The adult and child sit or stand side by side in close proximity to each other. 'Front-on' cuddle should be avoided for even without intent, face-to-face cuddle creates overtly sexual overtones. This enhances eye contact and gives some scope for both the adult and child to identify the body language which is taking place. Utterances and intonation of voice are also crucial here. The message the adult is giving, loud and clear, is 'it is quite safe to do this if you feel the need to, and, here is the boundary'.

This may sound rather sophisticated when thinking of our dealings with some adolescents. Whilst they may not be able to verbalise it as above, the message should be implicitly loud and clear in the response of the teacher. A further desirable to the above situation is to ensure that wherever possible the embrace described does not occur in a situation in which adult and child are alone. One benefit of a group being present is that it becomes more difficult for any allegations to be made. This allows the situation to be turned into a learning experience for all as well as a topic for subsequent discussion.

The sideways cuddle can be employed wherever circumstances arrive which involve a degree of touching. A major benefit of a 'sideways cuddle' is that disengagement can taken place without offence to those sharing the 'cuddle'. A gesture to move apart by either party is sufficient to disengage. Both parties should be able to identify the cues given by the other. If an occasion should arrive when a full embrace is encountered this should be reduced to a sideways cuddle immediately. This can easily be achieved by taking hold of one hand of the recipient and lowering it, at the same time turning so that both adult and child are facing in one direction.

It must be made quite clear, that to prolong a full embrace can only leave potential for problems. At one extreme is the potential for allegations to be made against the member of staff. At the other extreme, the child is left in considerable confusion as to what is acceptable and what it not. There is a need to clarify the situation not to add to the confusion of it.

There would appear to be an untapped source of information with respect to the concept of touch. Currently it is almost a taboo topic within schools due to the fear of allegations and misinterpretation of the contact between pupil and teacher. By distancing oneself from any contact, there is the knowledge of safety from allegations. Unfortunately, many children, possibly an increasing number of children, are denied appropriate experiences of touch. This dilemma needs to be addressed rather than banished.

The concern is that a significant number of children are now in residential educational establishments who are not only deprived of physical contact, but may have been deprived of appropriate touch for a vital period of time in their lives. It may be argued that it is right and correct that this is the case. Experience suggests that deficits here should be addressed and counter measures employed to permit some approved and supervised contact.

Children touching each other can be seen as a management problem. The fear is that what starts as horse play can escalate into something of a more serious nature. This is a pity, carefully supervised play fighting can be fun. The problems arise when it escalates into bullying or abuse of some nature. After all, isn't play fighting a part of growing up within the family at home?

Can attitudes be changed in residential educational establishments towards touch? Is it desirable that they should?

Who can or should be responsible for initiating such change? Should teachers be involved or not? Easy and safe answers may suggest that only carers should consider any of the above. There can still be no obligations. Some may argue that there is no case to make appropriate touch desirable anyway.

What of the teacher who is a houseparent? What of the teacher who is involved in 'extraneous duties'? Is there any scope for these to involve themselves?

It is suggested that all teachers should be more aware of the implications of what touch is all about. The positive as well as the negative implications. It is all the more important to consider implications of this for those who reside away from home. Can such an unrecognised need be addressed in those establishments. Should the houseparent or carer take positive steps to ensure that there is a potential for appropriate touch to happen? We are not talking about contact sports here. More ideas such as trust games, involving touching. Should the houseparent/carer go around tucking children into bed rather than shouting 'Lights out!' If so at what age should this stop? It happens in some homes well into the teenage years so why shouldn't it be appropriate to happen away from home? What lessons can be learned from the domestic staff or matron? Their knowledge of what is going on within the building is often second to none. They are frequently well respected by staff and pupils alike. Whilst staff infrequently come into physical contact with them, is that true of the pupils? Do they currently provide the shoulder to cry on, someone to hold on to, to cuddle, to be mothered by? If there is a shred of truth in this perhaps they offer an appropriate model which others may adopt or adapt, if it will contribute to the well-being of those children in residential educational establishments.

Positive touch initiated by a carer (it may not be initially perceived as positive by the recipient) in an appropriate manner may provide great comfort to a child. This is currently neglected in many school environments due to lack of ground rules and fear of being misinterpreted. Managers may provide initial safety measures to permit appropriate touch and these might include:

1) Ensuring that others are able to see what is happening.
2) Be sure to know the recipient sufficiently well that no offence can be construed from the encounter.
3) If an embrace takes place, this must be a sideways cuddle only.
4) The individual to feel no compulsion to touch. It must remain a deeply personal action. It is not wrong to touch, provided it is in the right circumstances.
5) Encounters which are initiated by a child should be shared with another colleague. This does not prevent an allegation being made subsequently, but if the incident is appropriately recorded and officially shared with an appropriate colleague, the event is made available professionally and honestly. This is good, professional child care, not merely self protection. This is contentious. It is in no way included to protect the offender. It does offer limited help to an innocent party who has an allegation made against them.

These five measures do not offer a complete answer. They do attempt to create a framework from which to start. All children who are away from home for whatever reason, should have the best care which is available. We continue to strive towards that end. Appropriate touch may have been increasingly neglected in recent times due to our preoccupation for self protection. Perhaps it is time to recognise that something extra is needed to that which we currently offer. Let's see if we can become more positive in facing up to the demands made upon us by the children who depend so totally upon our performance.

CHAPTER 10

Focus on Training Needs
Ewan Anderson

Introduction

In Britain, although there is a wide range of courses covering most facets of education, little training is available, specifically for those in boarding and residential education and care. Apart from the occasional short course, there is nothing at all for boarding staff. For other aspects of residential work, training must usually be obtained from units in more general courses. The best available are the various social work training courses and the Open University courses P653 (Caring for People and Young Children) and K254S (Working with Children and Young People). In the Open University packages there are units particularly targeted at those undertaking residential work. There is an obvious requirement, highlighted by the implementation of the Children Act, for a complete and coherent training programme for all those working with children in residential settings. As the inspection procedure for boarding schools and children's homes begins in earnest, this need will become increasingly more obvious.

There are several reasons for the lack of a common boarding and residential training programme. Most importantly, it has only been realised relatively recently that there was common ground, shared by practitioners in the diverse range of residential establishments for children. This realisation has, of course, received its major impetus through the introduction of the Children Act, in which the basic elements of good care, whatever the setting, are identified. It is hoped that this volume illustrates the point that, despite the obvious differences, there are more factors that unite rather than divide residential educators and trainers.

The lack of common training is also undoubtedly a result of differences in status. Where the two exist in the same establishment, care staff, whether trained or not, are almost invariably considered inferior to teaching staff. In the Social Services, residential child care officers tend to enjoy a status below that of field-workers. However, in many boarding schools, the housemaster or house-mistress, normally also a teacher, usually enjoys an exalted status within the hierarchy. Thus, boarding staff have tended to see little connection between their pastoral work and that of residential staff in special schools or children's homes. Nevertheless, all are dealing with children who, for one reason or another, are living away from home.

A third factor which has inhibited the development of common training has been the lack of recognition of residential work with children as a distinctive profession. In Britain, it has generally been viewed as an appendage to some other profession such as teaching, social work, nursing or psychiatry. In contrast, in many parts of the world, but particularly in Western Europe, the post of social educator, a person who educates children while living with them, is recognised. In sharing life with children, the social educator has many opportunities for caring, guidance, education, counselling and therapy. These elements provide the basis for the courses available in Western Europe, which are discussed in detail in the publications of the Federation Internationale des Communautes Educatives (FICE).

The present position

The general lack of training provision in all sectors of residential education in Britain means that most learning is carried out on the job. In independent boarding schools, a housemaster or house-mistress would, ideally, have been a house tutor first. Failing that, they would have been involved in some way with boarding or would possibly have been boarders themselves. However, such an apprenticeship system can clearly result in inbreeding and inertia, particularly obvious at a time when society is changing so rapidly. In contrast, a boarding community with several houses can provide support and generate new ideas. Nevertheless, many independent boarding schools and most maintained boarding schools have only one or perhaps two houses and therefore training through apprenticeship is rarely possible. Teachers with an inherent interest in boarding are unlikely to select such schools and thus there will be little accumulated boarding wisdom. In fact, it is increasingly true throughout boarding schools, that house staff with little experience are having to be appointed. In an attempt to overcome this problem, there have been a number of new initiatives. For instance, the Headmasters' Conference Schools have begun to develop a training programme. The Boarding Schools' Association has run a number of short courses and is considering a more substantial programme. One or two individual schools and groups of schools have begun co-ordinating residential training through regular discussions and INSET days. However, important as these developments are, since, through the Children Act, there is now a legal requirement for recognised good practice, they seem hardly sufficient. An agreed programme, accepted by both the Department of Health and the schools, broken down appropriately into units and courses, would be more effective. It would be available to all practitioners and would also provide a qualification.

In the special schools, assessment centres, children's homes and other elements of the residential education sector, there are some short courses available locally. However, as with the boarding sector, the vast majority of staff learn through on-job training. Some of the larger, voluntary, independent or non-maintained bodies have their own training programmes, but the effectiveness of these is likely to be related to the size of the organisation. Less specifically focused are the standard social-work training courses, designed essentially for field-workers. Residential social work demands a particular kind of dedication and, by the very nature of the work, periods of continuous attendance at courses are prohibited. Thus, the Open University programme is of particular value, but the two main courses include only limited elements on residential education and care. However, it is unlikely that the majority of residential workers will be able to receive training, other than through distance learning courses.

With the implementation of the Children Act it is vital that staff involved in boarding and other aspects of residential work with children receive training. Since, in the fields of education and social work, the number of staff is relatively very small, the best answer would seem to be a training programme designed for all residential staff. This could be taught in a variety of modes, including one-day courses, short courses, long courses, degree courses and distance-learning courses. Once established, the programme would facilitate the recognition of the professional status of the residential worker. Indeed, this might be considered the key reason for establishing such a training programme.

Training framework

Since the Children Act provides the context for training, guidance on the range of material to be included in the programme can be obtained from a report for the Social Services Inspectorate, Department of Health (*A Training Framework*, June 1991). This framework was designed with both boarding and residential workers and Social Service Department officers in mind. The proposed programme was divided into 22 units, each supported by a range of key reference material:

1) the Social Services;
2) the needs of children in residence;
3) the boarding school system;
4) a comparison between the different types of residential provision;
5) legislation: the statutory basis;
6) boarding need categories;
7) residential special needs;
8) boarding aims;
9) group living;
10) the boarding/pastoral system;
11) the residential environment;
12) boarding accommodation;
13) relationships and roles;
14) health and safety;
15) child protection;
16) control and discipline;
17) guidance and counselling;
18) religion and the cultural ethos;
19) documentation;
20) monitoring procedures;
21) conflicts in residence;
22) the inspection.

Given the necessity to implement training rapidly, the most appropriate approach was thought to be through self-tuition and local discussion groups, with the occasional lectures and seminars by visiting speakers. This was the mode adopted during the pilot studies for the Open University course P653 and the Holbrook Group itself has conducted a number of successful discussion sessions at different establishments. Whilst some schools would have sufficient staff to provide in-house training, the most effective group would probably be composed of staff from a variety of schools, boarding schools, special schools, assessment centres and other establishments for residential education or care provision. This would not only allow an interesting exchange of views, but would reinforce the concept of a common profession. The core of the programme, applicable throughout residential education and care would, for this programme, be provided by the Open University course P653.

However, if the professional status of the social educator is to be officially recognised, there would need to be a more structured and detailed framework, ranging from INSET days and short courses to diploma and degree courses. Such a framework could be organised according to the length of course, and level of study or the learning mode. On the other hand, it can probably be accepted that since the nature of residential posts poses obvious problems for training, the most effective strategy would be to provide as wide a variety of courses and approaches as possible. As a result, rather than produce a catalogue of possible courses, it seems more appropriate to adopt a developmental approach to the structuring of a training programme.

This approach is illustrated in Figure 6. At the core are the fundamental skills required by the social pedagogue in the practical setting. These are further enhanced through the various areas of residential education studies and are set in context within the appropriate academic fields. This approach not only prioritises the requirements, but also facilitates the construction of courses of varying length and differing levels.

On-job skills

The complete proposed programme has been discussed in detail with Social Service Department officers and practitioners across the entire range of boarding and residential education and care, but the main focus has been upon the practical skills required to ensure good practice on a day-to-day basis. These are thought to be the minimum requirements for a trained person. They would therefore provide the framework for induction courses, acquaint courses and day release or INSET day training. This is therefore the initial stage of training and the acquisition of these skills should be compulsory for all those involved in residential work with children.

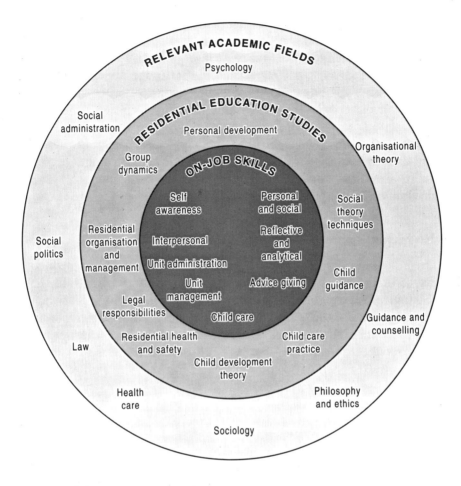

Figure 6   Structured training programme

Three groups of skills are required:

a)   those relating to the staff member personally;
b)   those required for dealing with children individually and in groups; and
c)   those necessary to ensure the smooth operation of the unit.

Self-awareness includes, in particular, the realisation that staff act as models and, for some children, it is in this capacity that they achieve their greatest effect. Skills needed for active work with children can be identified on various levels. Most basic are those concerned with the provision of primary care. Then there are those which relate to the personal and social development of the individual child and to advice giving. Beyond these are the skills required for working with groups and helping to foster interpersonal relationships. If this work is to be monitored and managed effectively, reflective and analytical skills are needed. If staff do not efficiently analyse and record the activity and behaviour within the unit, it is difficult to know whether progress towards the stated aims is being achieved. Other organisational skills are those related to management, including control and discipline, and to unit administration.

Residential education studies

On-job skills are essentially applied elements of studies which relate directly to residential education. Such studies provide the theoretical context and therefore greater understanding, which must enhance performance. Residential education studies would therefore form the basis for a certificate or diploma course lasting, perhaps, the equivalent of one year full-time. The course would be taken by staff who had acquired the on-job skills and a necessary period of practical experience.

Personal development would be studied to increase self awareness and therefore improve what might be termed the passive aspect of residential work. The effectiveness of active work with the children should be enhanced by studies of child care practice, child development theory, group dynamics and child guidance. A knowledge of social theory techniques would improve reflective and analytical skills and thereby the sophistication of the monitoring programme. The study of residential organisation and management, aspects of the law and elements of health and safety as related to residential living, would clearly affect the quality of unit administration and management.

Relevant academic fields

The residential education studies listed are themselves specially orientated parts of substantive academic fields. Thus, for a degree programme, the main units would be based upon each of these academic fields. Each of these can therefore be clearly related through residential education studies to the actual on-job skills needed for daily work in residence. The major contribution would come from psychology and sociology and there would be units in relevant aspects of guidance and counselling, social administration, social politics, organisational theory, law and health care.

Conclusion

If work with children living away from home is to be accorded professional status, it is essential that a coherent educational and training programme such as that described, is developed. The Children Act demands good practice throughout the field of boarding and residential education and care, and the basis for this is provided by the on-job skills. However, in order to attract staff of the highest quality and to facilitate career development, it is essential that certificate, diploma and degree courses are available and these can be constructed from and related directly to the on-job skill requirements. Work in specialised residential establishments would obviously require greater emphasis on some sectors of the training than others, but the programme outlined would offer a firm foundation for all those involved in residential work with children.

CHAPTER 11

The Dark Side of Boarding

David Robinson

Introduction

There is a type of abuse which, if not specific to boarding schools, is at least characteristic of them. This is the tyranny of the group which is seen when supervision is weak or, worse, when it is encouraged by those in charge. This is the subject of this chapter.

Boarding school, with its relative lack of privacy compared with home and its ready pooling of information amongst the children, offers some protection from the private, familial abuse that relies on secrecy and bizarre ideas of what constitutes right behaviour. Yet school-children are rightly afraid of being hurt and bullied.

In her book *Bullies and Victims in Schools* Valerie Besag wrote: 'A wide range of explanations has been offered for aggressive behaviour: decor, food additives, diet, medical conditions and, of course, previous experiences of all forms' (Besag, 1989). The view advanced here is that boys' potential for aggressive behaviour is innate and that boarding, to a greater or lesser extent, provides the conditions for its expression.

The Children Act seemed to concentrate at first on abuse of children by adults. A year ago North Yorkshire, in its *Child Abuse Guidelines*, paragraph 1.1, stated that

> it is generally accepted that an abused child is a child [under 17 who has suffered abuse] *which the person or persons who had custody, charge or care of the child either caused or knowingly failed to prevent.* (My italics)

It is to be welcomed that the definition seems to have broadened since, and *The Children Act 1989, Guidance and Regulations Volume 5, Independent Schools* (paragraph 2.2) makes no such qualification:

Schools should be aware that pupils may suffer physical, sexual or emotional abuse either whilst at home or away from the school, or within the school itself, by staff, other adults including parents, and other children.

The abuse which is considered in this chapter is a type of use, as the common root of *use, misuse* and *abuse* suggests. All these varieties of use convey the idea that one person or thing is *under the control or power* of another. Now the word 'bully' is defined as 'person who uses strength or power to coerce another by fear' (OED), and 'coerce' is in turn defined as 'forcibly constrain or impel [person] into obedience' (OED). Running these last two definitions together we have bully defined as 'person who uses force to constrain or impel another into obedience by fear'. The Guidance and Regulations further state in 3.9.2(b) 'Where senior pupils have a degree of authority over others, it must be clear that there is no exploitation of one pupil by another.' 'Exploitation' is defined as 'utilisation of person, etc. for one's own ends'. Lastly, *The Children Act 1989, The Welfare of Children in Boarding Schools Practice Guide* states in paragraph 6.7 the principle that 'abuse, in whatever form, always constitutes serious harm to the child'. Based upon this constellation of definitions the definition of abuse which will be used in this chapter is 'the use of another for the abuser's own ends, to the detriment of the abused'.

What follows is designed to be thought provoking rather than definitive. Much more should be written about the positive aspects of boarding. But this chapter is about the dark side.

Boarding school

Residential care attempts to substitute for family life and even parents. An attempt is made to reclaim the child, to compensate for past deprivation. The emphasis is on emotional nurture and on a 'decelerating environment' (see Davison, Chapter 6).

Boarding is different from both family life and residential care. The ideal starting point (though it cannot be assumed) is that the bond between child and parents is good, that the child feels assured of their love, and that school for part of the year is an opportunity for greater personal knowledge and growth than could be achieved at home. It promotes rapid socialisation, selflessness, awareness of others' rights, self-control and understanding of human nature, by providing potential friends of the same age who are likely to share the child's interests. In Davison's terms the emphasis is on acceleration, not deceleration. Two differences between boarding life and family life are of particular interest. First, the adult/child ratio is vastly different; as a boarder the child will be one of a large group of children. Second, contrasting 19th-century school and family, Fitch commented:

> It is not well to make believe that a school, even a small school, is a family, because it is not one.... The moral basis of family life is affection. The moral basis of school life, as of all large communities, is justice. (Fitch, 1895)

A child cannot rely on that love from the staff of a boarding school as he or she might expect from his or her parents.

At this point it is worth pausing to consider two particular influences on the structure of a boarding school. One is the legacy of the monasteries and the church (in view of the religious foundations of many of our schools), the other the more human, pragmatic and personal input of the adults who are in charge and the children who make up the group. An institution requires rules for its smooth running, but there are Rules and rules.

Although monasteries are far removed from today's schools, they were for centuries the only place of learning that existed. That they may still have an influence may be surmised from the religious foundations of many of our schools, and is evidenced by the word 'carrel', for example, which in some schools means a space for private study but which originally meant a small enclosure in a monastery. Those in monasteries were subject to a Rule such as the Rule of St Benedict which emphasised obedience and humility, essential ingredients for the well-ordered society. Monastery itself derives from the Greek *monos* (alone) and monastic means 'pertaining to the solitary life'. These notions of obedience, humility and solitude contrast sharply with the independence, price and corporate life cultivated in many schools today.

It is to be doubted whether St Benedict's Rule, which informed monastic life for a millennium, could have survived the Children Act. Chapter 30 tells how boys are to be saved from excommunication, hell and the loss of their souls:

> Disciplinary measures should be appropriate to every age and intelligence; hence when boys or youths or others, incapable

of understanding how serious a punishment excommunication is, commit offences, such persons are to suffer additional fasts or painful stripes, so that they may be cured.

This is in line with the proverbial 'He that spareth his rod hateth his son, but he that loveth him chasteneth him betimes' (Proverbs 13, v. 24). The distinction the religious make between body and soul is further illustrated by St Francis of Assisi, who as he was dying apologised to his body, 'poor brother donkey', for having abused it so much.

The Children Act may be more concerned for the corporeal health of children than their souls. But the point to be made here is that in departing from a published Rule which all lived under, the way is open to individuals to pursue their own ends, openly or covertly, in running their school or house. The Children Act rightly requires that a formal policy is published and available for inspection by parents and pupils.

Groups

The initial task for a new boarder is to settle in, and during the first term parents appreciate hearing that he or she 'has made some good friends'; in the absence of this reassurance the housemaster's comment that their child 'is independent' may sound vague warning bells. All new pupils to some extent have to adopt the mores of their new society if they are to be accepted, even if this means rejecting old values. Though the humiliating initiation ceremonies of the last century, which had the effect of stripping entrants of their separate personal dignity, may have gone, there is still an element of breaking and reforming of the new entrant's character. A girls' boarding school, priding itself on its friendliness, thoughtfully allocates an older pupil to each new girl to ease her entry into the school. That the new girl is called the 'nut', and her aide the 'nut-cracker' is a revealing comment on the nature of the process.

Parents need to be assured that the values to which the sensitive kernel of their child will be exposed will be a good influence. Perhaps one of greatest assets of a good boarding school lies in its ability to select pupils, and in its reserving the right to remove those who are found to be unsuitable. Thomas Arnold made it a condition of his appointment at Rugby that he had absolute power to remove children from the school. 'Till a man learns that the first, second, and third duty of a schoolmaster is to get rid of unpromising subjects, a great public school', he said, 'will never be what it might be, and what it ought to be' (Stanley, 1904). Making the same point, but conversely, residential homes which are places of last resort for children can become worse environments if, in addition to their abused and neglected children they are required to take young people on remand for theft and assault when there is no suitable accommodation in prisons.

A group can take on a life of its own, greater than the sum of its members, emboldening some and inhibiting others. Elias Canetti, whose acute observations of crowds in Europe during Hitler's rise to power in the 1930s were the basis for his book *Crowds and Power* included 'equality' amongst his four attributes which a crowd always possessed:

> *Within the crowd there is equality.* This is absolute and indisputable and never questioned by the crowd itself. It is of fundamental importance and one might even define a crowd as a state of absolute equality. A head is a head, an arm is an arm, and differences between individual heads and arms are irrelevant. It is for the sake of this equality that people become a crowd and they tend to overlook anything which might detract from it. All demands for justice and all theories of equality ultimately derive their energy from the actual experience of equality familiar to anyone who has been part of a crowd. (Canetti, 1962)

One might add that there is also security and power within the crowd. But there is a price to be paid. Dissimilar views, opinions and judgements are ridiculed, perhaps to ensure that they disappear, perhaps to reject their possessor, perhaps to confirm and strengthen the group's own values, perhaps for all three reasons. Signs of selfishness or difference are sought for as the newcomer is rated and given his rank in the school. Undue attachment to possessions and lack of faith in the group are elicited as his bag is thrown around the room. Though natural academic ability is grudgingly accepted, a child who gains advantage over his fellows by working harder than average tends to be despised. There is a natural, instinctive and occasionally formulated justice at work and sometimes children stopped from tormenting another will defend themselves by saying 'We were teaching him a lesson', and may add 'It is for his own good.' They mean it.

Richard Dawkins has suggested in *The Selfish Gene* (Dawkins, 1976) that there is a biological altruism which depends on degree of relatedness: the more closely related one is to someone, the more one will act to help him or her. Survival of the genes which are borne in common is his explanation of unselfish behaviour which can extend to self-sacrifice for the sake of another. This help diminishes as the proportion of genes in common, so that siblings will receive more help from each other than will cousins. He supports this thesis with detailed research across the animal kingdom. The importance of blood ties has always been accepted in human society; most recently, during the Gulf War, we heard the Arabic saying 'cousin against cousin but cousins against the Americans'. It is tempting to wonder whether there might be a genetic basis for the requirement of similarity or likeness which close groups impose upon their members.

Yet it seems that mankind is capable of having honorary brothers and sisters, those whom the American Indians, as if anticipating Dawkins, called blood brothers. Such relationships divide as well as unite people and it is interesting that school uniforms are designed as much to cover up differences between those who wear them as to emphasise their differentness from those who wear a different uniform. It seems that members of a group should be similar to each other, but different from those in other groups.

Much group pressure appears designed to remove differences and, in particular, what the group sees as selfishness. It may be a truism that nothing burns in hell but self-will, but it is still hell for a child who clings to self-will. Two popular and well-adjusted sixth-form boarders at two schools have told me how they had been unhappy earlier. One had had a bleak fifth year, an outcast from his group, but commented that 'it was all my own fault', and had regained his popularity since. The other had had a very difficult first few years, at loggerheads with everyone, but then he had 'seen the light', and was now enjoying school greatly.

There is an uncomfortable parallel with conditioning. A boarding school can threaten a child's integrity, that bundle of attitudes and responses already present by a mixture of heredity and family environment when the child enters school. The idea of integrity is a difficult one. Its Latin root is *integer*, whole, untouched, unhurt, complete, entire. That one can retain, preserve or lose one's integrity, but not find it suggests that it is a possession from birth, consistent with its Latin root. Integrity is generally reckoned an asset, but schoolchildren know that a companion blessed with an almost divine sense of certainty, an inflexible will, an uncompromising truthfulness, and a supreme lack of understanding of the world as they know it is a thorn in their sides nevertheless. Such a child's integrity will cost him dearly, and yet if in the end he accepts a more realistic and comfortable view of life it may be said that he has lost his integrity. One can understand why parents who hold minority beliefs sometimes seek a 'guarded' education for their children.

It is often said that boys who have boarded show emotion less than those who have not. The 'stiff upper lip' in times of stress has been viewed by some as a valuable characteristic of the ex-public schoolboy, whilst others see a lamentable atrophy of important emotions which have been denied expression for too long.

Any child sent to an inappropriate school is at risk, and the danger is increased when the school is a boarding school. As an example, consider the child of limited academic ability sent by ambitious parents to attend an academic school where he hardly understands the lessons and who comes bottom of his class year after year, whilst his sunny disposition changes to a sense of worthlessness. Or consider a similar child who, rather than settle for total defeat, begins to disrupt lessons and bully. Or consider the weak child in a school where sports, strength and physical prowess count for everything. Children need to find an area where they can succeed, and a school which strives overmuch to maximise children's potential in a particular field must reject those whose nature is unsuitable.

Occasionally a child is rejected by the group as well as the school. Like the one chicken in the run which has lost most of its feathers, he or she wanders around in a daze, unable to contribute appropriately to any communal activity. Shame at what they have come to understand is their own inadequacy, and the armour which they develop under such circumstances can even make such children reply 'fine' whenever they are asked how they are. For a boarder the isolation that results may be a *double* isolation, isolation from family as well as those around, as noted in the *Practice Guide*, paragraph 6.47. Such children are mercifully rare.

Lastly, the arrival of girls at a hitherto exclusively male boarding school must be considered: they are generally judged to exert a positive and beneficial influence. It may be that boys are non-plussed to some extent by their arrival, insofar as they are a group which refuses to engage in the competitive and aggressive behaviour which characterises a purely boys' society. They present an alternative *modus vivendi* and, as they grow up, individual attractions which draw members away from the male group. Sixth formers at one public school lamented the loss of friends in this way as CBM – Chicks Before Mates. Girls deserve consideration as a separate group.

Girls

A mixed school *feels* smaller than its overall numbers would suggest if it were all boys; it is as if the girls and boys form different constituencies. A group imposes the condition of similarity on its members, and girls are demonstrably dissimilar from boys in appearance and dress. Moreover, insofar as part of the motivation for boys joining a group may be to affirm their identity with others in that group, and insofar as gender is part of that identity, there may be a disinclination, particularly by young children, to play with children of the opposite sex. Yet even this may be somewhat contentious as an explanation.

More fundamentally it seems that there is a difference in *valency* between boys and girls in their friendships, to use a chemical simile. Boys can be characterised as *multi-valent*, forming attachment to many others in the group and in consequence capable of forming large coherent groups, as discussed earlier. Girls, on the other hand, seem to be more *mono-valent*, often preferring a best friend to membership of a gang. Though girls do form groups, it seems that the bonds between girls in these groups are more intense than bonds between boys. Whilst girls seek *best* friends, boys are happy with *good* friends. This may be the essential difference between boys and girls in the context of groups.

To carry the chemical analogy one step further, one can imagine a group of (multivalent) boys as forming a single rather sticky and reactive molecule, with each boy forming bonds in every direction and not caring too much about which *particular* people are included in his bonds so long as they are members of the group. The edges of this group would have valency free for including others. A group of (monovalent) girls might be imagined as a loose assembly of diatomic molecules. The reaction between the boys' and girls' molecules could be imagined as single attachments which weaken a boy's multivalency and so cohesion of the large molecule or group with, in the limit, the boy – girl molecule breaking off from the large group. This is, of course, a gross simplification but it illustrates the idea.

In a lecture delivered in 1880, Joshua Fitch (HMI of Training Colleges) said:

> A big conventional boarding house for girls is unlike any world which they are ever likely to enter. It has no lesson to teach and no discipline to furnish, which bears at all on the future claims of society and of home. Hence while the ideal boarding school for boys may be large and stately; with its strong sense of corporate unity, its traditions, its contests, its publicity, its representation on a small scale of municipal and political life; the ideal boarding school for girls is an institution large enough indeed as to all its teaching arrangements ... but organised as to all its domestic arrangements, on the principle of small sheltered boarding-houses in separate communities of not more than 20, each under the care of a mistress who shall stand *in loco parentis*. And in each of such boarding-houses it is well that care should be taken to gather together under the same roof scholars of very different ages, in order that relations of helpfulness and protection may be established between the elder and the younger, and that in this way something analogous to the natural discipline of a family may be attained. (Fitch, 1895)

It would be interesting to compare Fitch's prescription for girls boarding in 1880 with the current trend towards smaller and more familial houses for boys, and to ask to what extent the trend is due to the wish for parity between boys and girls, to increasing affluence, and to a move away from the idea of boarding as a preparation for political society to the idea of boarding being a replacement for home. But this would take us far beyond the scope of this chapter.

It has been suggested that the rationale for boys' boarding is the opportunity it provides for group life, and all that entails. But if girls tend to be monovalent then they will benefit less from the multi-bonding opportunities of boarding. Girls' problems seem to centre on personal attachments, and jealousy and victimisation within small groups of half a dozen. Whilst boys generally accept bedroom allocation stoically, girls are far more fussy about whom they will and will not share with – and develop sudden likes and aversions. Girls may stand to gain less than boys from boarding.

Boys outnumber girls in boarding schools. In their January 1992 census, ISIS found 60,302 boys and 37,369 girls in independent boarding schools in this country. A weak reason for the relative unpopularity of girls' boarding compared with boys' is that parents do not value daughters' education as highly as that of their sons. But, following the argument above, it is possible that the imbalance is because the average girl is less suited to, and actually gets less benefit from, life in an extended community than the average boy. One might, on this model, expect the numbers to equalise only when the sole reason for boarding is necessity.

One last observation on the differences between boy and girl boarders is that apart from those girl boarders who genuinely choose to board, and so might be more multivalent than girls as a whole, there are others who board out of necessity. Many in this latter group might be expected to require especial support and attention from house staff if they are not to suffer unduly in what, for some of them at least, is likely to prove a particularly alien environment.

Domains

Girls will be left behind as we move to consider territory. Tiger, before spending 30 pages of his book *Men in Groups* detailing and lamenting the rarity of women in politics, observed 'On the question of territoriality, it may be wisest to accept Lowie's cautious formulation that territoriality and male groups are the basis of political activity' (Tiger, 1970). Let us now consider the new boy at boarding school.

Gradually he finds that his peers share his fears, anxieties, hopes and aims and he realises that they, however different their public façade, have a great deal in common with him. I will use the term 'world' to mean the collection of things that are significant to a person. Communal life tends to align the boarders' personal worlds so that they will to some extent share the same values, aims and perspectives.

But just as the new boy is realising his sameness, he is also realising the depth of the differences too. Even those who share his experiences perceive them differently, notice different things, and may be oblivious to that which seems most significant to him. People's worlds are different, as are their attitudes to them. Take as examples two children who inhabit worlds which are different in *quality*.

First there is the child whose world is the people around him, who cannot think of himself separate from his friends and relatives. One such boarder found weekends extremely hard to bear. His friends were weekly boarders who went home every weekend. It was as if part of him was being amputated every Saturday, such was the slough of despond he was plunged into, and repeated separation did not inure him to the loss. Some Sundays he felt 'almost suicidal'. Provision of more activities at weekends might have distracted him from his loss and lessened his depression.

Second consider the boy whose world may be largely empty of those round about, who has plenty of ideas and has plenty to do. Quiet and independent, he may welcome the weekends as a chance to do his own thing without the pressure of others. He may have considerable control over his world, but no desire to influence other people whom he may regard as sovereign wills, like his own. By the same token he resents interference from others. Boarding is likely to socialise such a person to some extent.

A person's world is their sphere of involvement and defines their field of action. I will use the word 'domain' to refer to that subset of his world which a boy would reckon to own, to have a degree of power over. It is a generalised form of Ardrey's 'territory', which he defines as 'an area of space, whether of water or earth or air, which an animal or group of animals defends as an exclusive preserve' (Ardrey, 1967). Domains are not limited to physical space; depending on the worlds which they are subsets of they may contain objects, ideas, skills or other people, as well as space.

To the extent that a new boy fits in, his domain will complement the domains of others, and if domains overlap it must be with mutual consent if people are to live together in harmony. Yet a person's domain would appear to be an expanding subset of their world, at least until the infirmities of old age diminish it, and there is a tendency for a young person's domain to fill the space available. A worthwhile domain gives its possessor self-esteem, and status too insofar as the domain is valued by others.

The child whose world consists of appetites and possessions, whose attitude is selfish and greedy and who has little conception of the sovereignty of other's domains, is a real problem in a boarding community. He may be oblivious to the damage he does, and can be characterised as a thief as he expands his domain with others' goods. If not carefully watched, such a person will shamelessly appropriate communal resources. There will be no more cake than there was before, and the selfishness of this one person will cause others to grab things too in order to get their share. Such people say to those who go without: 'You should have come earlier or spoken up louder; in any case, you must look out for yourself.' The weaker fail to get their ration, and the fatness of some does not compensate for the death of the community.

Bullies delight in the exercise and expansion of their power. Possessed of an almost insatiable desire to assert themselves, it is almost as if they act from insecurity, an assumption that others are as predatory as themselves. An almost infallible way for a new boy to fall foul of the group is to lay claim to more power or knowledge than the group is ready to accord him. If the child persists then he is likely to be victimised by the group; that such victims make real bullies when they are bigger may not be a direct result of having been bullied (though it may increase their wish to bully and be advanced as an explanation), but a consequence of the same wish to control others has led to their being bullied when they were younger. Pure bullying must humiliate the victim; the clearer it is that the victim is of no significance to the bully, the more successful the bully has been. The purpose is a demonstration of power and a warning to others: 'Humour me, or this might happen to you.' The more successful bully will also use rewards to reinforce his message, and unexpectedly take interest in people, talking warmly to them as if to say 'Humour me and I will be nice to you.' The bully cannot have fear of him drive people away: he must keep them close if he is to continue to assert himself.

Bullying rarely involves the physical beating of one small boy by another, larger boy, for this is likely to provoke the wrath of the bully's peers against the bully, in defence of the underdog and under the precept of fair play. The assertion of superiority is far more easily and acceptably done by belittling others, by selectively ignoring them, by public body language which shows that the victim is really of no significance. This is also the natural way in which power is communicated and the boarder, unlike a day pupil, has little escape if on the receiving end.

The socially weakest, however, may be weak simply because they have few pretensions in the social world. Their domain, even their world, may be largely disjointed from other peoples', and it is as well for their self-esteem that this is so, though if their world is disjointed from the social world it would explain their low status there. Some children, indeed, specialise in such domains, in worlds which invite little competition from others. Examples are esoteric areas of expert knowledge, minority sports, and collections. Stamp collecting is a particularly interesting hobby in this respect. The stamps are objects totally under control of the collector, who decides which to collect, discard and swap and how they are arranged in his album. The tiny pieces of paper represent countries and their album the world. This domain is tantamount to real territory, and must suffice until the child grows stronger.

Such domains, sublimations of real territory, are the salvation of the socially weak. The child who appears isolated after his arrival at school may become quiet, waiting, biding his time, whilst exploring new worlds, new potential domains. All boarders agree that life gets better as they become more senior in the school, but it is *they* who get better at ameliorating their lot, at finding domains where they can grow.

Leaders

A small boy who has a black eye has undoubtedly been hurt, but has he been *abused*? He may have been hit accidentally by a golf ball. He may have fought with a boy of the same size, each suffering equal black eyes until they were stopped. Or he may have been beaten up by a bigger boy. I would argue that only this last can be abuse, and that a difference in power, a *power differential*, is a precondition for abuse.

It is said that power tends to corrupt. It is reasonable to suppose that the danger increases in proportion to the power differential between people. One might expect, therefore, to see less abuse where the power differential is less: in single age boarding houses, amongst senior houses in general. Conversely there would be greater scope for abuse by adults where their charges are young, mentally handicapped, disadvantaged, inarticulate, frightened and/or possessed of low self-esteem. Adults who care for others need to be alert to this danger.

Adults charged with pastoral care of children have a complex responsibility, being both masters and servants of those in their care. There is a biological paradigm of all-powerful service in parenthood, and we all possess an instinct to care for and to help the weak and defenceless – so long as we feel a relationship with them. The master can even become subservient to the needs and demands of those cared for: the exigencies of a housemaster's job has led at least one to picture himself as a dog in a kennel, chained to his house and those in his care.

Insofar as the community is a group, it can be ruled by a single leader. This susceptibility is both the strength and potential weakness of boarding. It is its strength because it enables a good and strong housemaster to inspire his children with coherent and moral aims and ideals. The more absolute his power, the stronger his influence. The good man will resist the temptation to be corrupted by this power into delusions of being even a demi-god. But this concentration of power is a weakness if the person in authority is a shrewd despot, appearing to honour the rules under which he was appointed but running an entirely different establishment which is kept secret by fear or, if made known, by disbelief. The case of Crookham Court is, if not unique, very much an exception, but it makes the point. Such a situation can occur anywhere in the hierarchy of command if a particular person is not adequately monitored, and in particular it might occur amongst loosely supervised prefects.

Yet if prefects are supervised too closely their job ceases to have any meaning. The purpose of appointing senior pupils to posts of responsibility is to inculcate a sense of responsibility in the role models both to aid their personal growth and also so that they will be more worthy exemplars. It entails the possibility – even the probability – that mistakes will be made and the housemaster, taking care to monitor the situation carefully, will find occasions when he must question his support for his prefects and decide when, and how, to intervene. And he must intervene at times.

It is worth considering why someone becomes a teacher, a carer, a housemaster or housemistress. To what extent is *power* over an impressionable audience sought? To what extent does he or she want to *serve* those cared for? He or she will have a dark side too. It is traditional that caring professionals are paid less than their non-caring peers, and it may be a case of virtue or job satisfaction being its own reward. But another factor is the power that they are given over others: nurses and doctors over patients, teachers over children. Where those who are helped are most powerless – the very young, the mentally and physically handicapped, the ill, the dying – the power differential is greatest. Is the power they are given over others an incentive in itself and another compensation for low pay?

The concepts of using and serving people can be confused. Thomas Arnold, Headmaster of Rugby, was, according to John Chandos (1984),

> as egoist tormented by a will which craved to impose itself remedially, as he supposed, upon others.... To Arnold this painful process was 'love', for 'My love of any place or person, or institution, is exactly the measure of my desire to reform them.' In unguarded moments of exhilaration he betrayed the true nature of his feelings and view of himself. 'The work here ... I like it better and better; because it has all the interest of a great game of chess, with living creatures for pawns *and pieces, and your adversary, in plain English, the Devil: truly he plays a very tough game, and is very hard to beat, if I ever do beat him.'*

(I have added in italics the end of Arnold's sentence, written in a letter to F. Hartwell in 1830, but not quoted by Chandos.) Arnold found that making prefects of his academic elite did not work. The only effective leaders amongst the pupils, he found, were the sportsmen.

Now sports teams are real shadows of hunting packs. Participation is conditional on competence, and team members, though they may have different functions, gain equality. It is a close, multivalent relationship: all are necessary. Boys tend to form such groups spontaneously and it is likely that if schools did not referee and umpire games according to published rules then something similar would happen anyway, but according to the nature of street gangs.

There is a desire for success and power − and a fear of being left out − amongst team members. The monastic virtues of humility and obedience may still be present at a personal level (though modesty may be more appropriate than humility) but at the team level there is likely to be pride and aggression. There is enormous energy here, and it may be that one of the greatest achievements of English public schools in the last century was to harness this energy and, by careful counselling of the team captains, imbue them and their followers in and beyond the team with notions of fair play. But it is a difficult task. Too weak a stewardship of games captains may always allow the natural selfishness of the dark side to surface, and favouritism and effect to overcome fairness and reason.

The dark side

The importance of non-verbal communication is being recognised though we have become largely unconscious of the messages sent and received. Such vital communication predates speech in our evolutionary history. At the risk of oversimplification and exceptions, much of the group behaviour of boys seems to be the expression of an atavistic way of life which would appear to have favoured survival at a time when men went out to hunt whilst women stayed at home to look after children. If the properties of boy groups are compared with those of hunting packs, it appears that they are properties which aid survival and so would have been transmitted to us through natural selection.

- Boys seek to maximise their domain, their territory.
- Boys seek to compete. They seek to be strongest themselves for the strongest do as they please, even in the domains of the rest of the group.
- Boys form groups. Mutual help confers great survival advantage.
- Boys are multivalent in their relationships. There is a taboo on sentiment and on exclusive friendships, for a member of a pack must owe allegiance to all.

Girls in boarding schools seem to be subject to their own set of instinctive imperatives.

- Girls' friendships are intense, more one-to-one than boys'. Is this a remnant of their role as mothers, with much greater responsibility for their *own* children than others'? The genes of mothers who cared for all children equally would not be transmitted as surely as those of mothers who cared only for their own.
- Girls exhibit far greater empathy than boys. Hysteria (from the Greek for the womb) used to be thought a purely female condition until the last century; nevertheless the British Medical Association notes that mass hysteria (the spread of, for example, fainting) 'usually occurs in schools or institutions of young women' (BMA, 1990). What possible survival value could this have? It would seem to be a side effect of that empathy which gives children of mothers who

possess it a greater chance of surviving than those whose mothers do not. Certainly men who faint in battle stand less chance of fathering children than those who do not, and one can at least understand the weakening of this characteristic amongst men.

- Girls menstrual cycles synchronise when living together. Could this be an echo of a time in the past when the men regularly left the women behind whilst they went off to hunt?

Such characteristics are instinctive, spontaneous and unconscious. They are dark because they fall outside the light of consciousness. And, insofar as reason is conscious, they also lie outside the sphere of reason. The dark side pervades all aspects of our lives, so much part of them that it is all but invisible, unremarked on because ever present. Yet it is vital to remark on it because although its promptings conferred survival value during the long hunter – gatherer phase of human evolution, they may not be appropriate in more modern communities. Its impulses lead us *blindly*, its patterns of behaviour remaining unconscious, awakened and exercised but not considered or chosen.

It is clear that if natural selection has handed the dark side to use then its mores are those of self-interest, and that apparent altruism that I have called corporate self-interest. Now the backbone of every moral and ethical code is self-denial. Schrödinger wrote that in order for morality to overcome our primitive nature we must begin by illuminating that nature and become aware of the tensions that are revealed (Schrödinger, 1959). One is reminded, perhaps, of Arnold who was keenly aware of the good and evil in people and who once wrote that schoolmastering was like a game of chess with the Devil. The dark side must be illuminated if our inner nature is to change and reflect values more appropriate to civilised society than to warring tribes.

Boarding can very easily become an education in, and an evocation of, the dark side. Adults as well as children are subject to its imperatives. Boarders generally become very conversant with the skills of group life, and boarding is rightly prized as a character-building challenge, as good training for life in a competitive world. But the hunter gatherer has no sentiment for the useless member of the group, or for someone who appears so different as to belong to a different group. Some suffering can lead a child to a more worthwhile and productive life. But there is also suffering which serves no purpose but to gratify those inflicting it. This is real child abuse. Its motives stem from our deeper animal nature, from an atavistic need for power or status. Child abuse particularly offends our moral sense because of the special protection we rightly afford the young, but it has the same character as an assault by one adult, or group of adults, on another. The dark side of boarding is simply the dark side of society. House spirit is not so far removed from nationalistic pride or religious fervour that a connection cannot be seen, and the mechanisms that group people into warring factions, lamentably evident in the world today and throughout history, can occasionally be seen in the boarding school.

So those who are appointed to positions of responsibility in boarding houses should be aware of the implications of the dark side for both themselves and their charges. Those who board must be carefully selected and well supervised. Those who would act as leaders of a pack, as seed crystals of such a crowd, who have a constant need to assert and demonstrate superiority and to need followers, those natural leaders, need to be attended to very closely. Though they may reach exalted positions in a competitive world, though they may be relied upon to follow a powerful housemaster's orders to the letter, they may worship power rather than reason, and might rather than right. Their good behaviour in front of authorities whom they respect is not a cause for complacency. Likewise those who are natural victims need close support and protection whilst they build their self-esteem and find success somewhere. It is when supervision fails, or the adults in charge are possessed of a need to use children for their own ends, that the dark side of boarding develops into real evil.

Whilst we continue to be ruled by emotions rather than reason, a moral atmosphere is needed to combat the selfishness that is at the heart of the dark side. Though corporate self-interest is arguably better than pure self-interest it must be distinguished from genuine altruism. The essential message or religions lies not in their disjoint creeds which invite both belief and enmity, but in their common core. It has been said that the most religious place in Europe is the particle accelerator at CERN, where the physicists engaged in high energy particle physics have an informed knowledge of the essential unity underlying the Universe, The message that 'All is One' is too prosaic to be enlightening; John Donne puts it better in his famous passage 'No man is an island' and the message must be restated often for it is the rational and mystical basis for understanding which makes child abuse – and war – the irrational and immoral crime that it is.

No man is an *Iland*, intire of it selfe; every man is a peece of the *Continent*, a part of the *maine*; if a *Clod* bee washed away by the *Sea, Europe* is the lesse, as well as if a *Promontorie* were, as well as if a *Mannor* of thy friends or of *thine owne* were; any mans *death* diminishes *me*, because I am involved in *Mankinde*; And therefore never send to know for whom the *bell* tolls; It tolls for *thee*. (Donne, 1936)

References

Anderson, E.W. (1975) 'Boarding Objectives', *Boarding Education* 2. London: Boarding Schools Association.

Anderson, E.W. (1978) *Assessment of Boarding*, Boarding Schools Association Occasional Paper 4. London: Boarding Schools Association.

Anderson, E.W. (1979a) *Kenton Lodge School Residential Research Report Number One*. University of Newcastle upon Tyne.

Anderson, E.W. (1979b) 'Residential Education Research Project', *Research Topics 3*. University of Newcastle upon Tyne.

Anderson, E.W. (1981) *Kenton Lodge School Residential Research Report Number Two*. University of Newcastle upon Tyne.

Anderson, E.W. (1990) 'The Aims of Boarding', *Boarding Education* 16.

An Introduction to the Children Act 1989 (1991) London: HMSO.

Appleyard, D. (1969) 'City Designers and the Pluralistic City', in L. Rodwin, *et al. Regional Planning for Development*. Cambridge, Mass.: MIT Press University Press Stanford.

Ardrey, R. (1967) *The Territorial Imperative*. London: Collins.

Argyle, M. (1969) *Social Interaction*. London: Methuen.

Barker, R. (1968) *Ecological Psychology*. Stanford: Stanford University Press.

Berry, J. (1989) 'Daily Experience in Residential Care', in eds S. Morgan and P. Righton *Child Care: Concerns and Conflicts*. London: Open University/Hodder and Stoughton.

Besag, V. (1989) *Bullies and Victims in Schools*. Milton Keynes: Open University Press.

Billington, R. (1991) 'The Lure of the Blackboard Jungle', *Daily Telegraph*, 7 March

Bloom, B.S. (1956) *Taxonomy of Educational Objectives: Cognitive Domain*. New York: David McKay.

Boarding in Maintained Schools: A Survey (a report by HMI) (1990) London: DES.

Boarding School Line. A Summary of the Results of an Experimental Helpline for Boarding School Pupils, January – July 1991. (1992) London: DES.

Bowlby, J. (1951) *Maternal Care and Mental Health*. World Health Organization. London: HMSO.

Bowlby, J. (1969, 1973, 1980) *Attachment and Loss* vols 1–3. London: Hogarth Press and Penguin.

Bowlby, J. (1988) *A Secure Base*. London: Tavistock/Routledge.

Brown, R. (1988) *Group Processes – Dynamics Within and Between Groups*. Oxford: Blackwell.

British Medical Association (1990) *Complete Family Health Encyclopaedia*. London: Dorling Kindersley.

Callow, M. (1988) *A Case Study of the Problems of Transition to Life in a Boys'*

Boarding School. Unpublished M.A. dissertation, University of East Anglia.

Canetti, E. (1962) *Crowds and Power.* London: Gollancz.

Canter, D. and Canter, S. (eds) (1979) *Designing for Therapeutic Environments.* London: Wiley.

Central Council for Education and Training in Social work (1978) *Good Enough Parenting.* CCETSW.

Chandos, J. (1984) *Boys Together English Public Schools 1880–1864.* London: Hutchinson.

Child Abuse Guide-lines. North Yorkshire. SSD, North Allerton.

Council of Local Education Authorities (1990) *Draft Curriculum Statement.* CLEA.

Davison, A.J. (1984) *'Triple Losers'. A Study of the Failing of Adolescent Girls in Residential Establishments, with Special Reference to Self Destructive Behaviour amongst Girls Exhibiting Extreme Handling Problems.* Unpublished DAES dissertation, University of Newcastle upon Tyne.

Davison, A.J. (1985) *Stress as a Component of an Interactional Institutional Climate. A Discussion and Case Study.* Unpublished B. Phil. dissertation, University of Newcastle upon Tyne.

Davison, A.J. (1989) *Representational Reality: The Role of Mental Models in Child Care. The Iconic Interactional Module Systems Approach to Working with Children in Group Care.* Unpublished Ph.D. dissertation. University of Newcastle upon Tyne.

Davison, A.J. (1990) *The Power/Authority Component of Residential/Boarding Establishments.* Holbrook Group Report II.

Dawkins, R. (1976) *The Selfish Gene.* Oxford: Oxford University Press.

Department of Education and Science (1989) *Personal and Social Education from 5 to 16.* London: HMSO.

Department of Health *Homes are for Living in.* London: DOH, HMSO.

Department of Health and Morgan, R. (1992) *School Life: Pupil Based Standards in Boarding Schools.* London: HMSO.

Department of Health (1991) *The Children Act 1989. The Welfare of Children in Boarding Schools, Practice Guide.* London: DOH, SSI, HMSO.

Donne, J. (1936) *Complete Poetry and Selected Prose.* London: The Nonesuch Press.

Eraut, M. (1973) *Support Materials for Courses in Educational Technology. Module 5: Evaluation.* National Council for Educational Technology.

Fisher, S. (1991) 'Homesickness and Health at Boarding Schools', chapter 5 in ed. G. Walford *Private Schooling.* Paul Chapman Publishing Ltd.

Fitch, J.G. (1895) *Lectures on Teaching.* Cambridge: Cambridge University Press.

Flekoy, M.A. (1991) *A Voice for Children. Speaking Out as Their Ombudsman.* UNICEF. London: Jessica Kingsley Publishers.

Friedman, A., Zimring, C. and Zube, E. (1978) *Environmental Design Evaluation.* New York: Plenum.

Gathorne-Hardy, J. (1977) *The Public School Phenomenon.* London: Hodder and Stoughton.

The Education (Standards for School Premises) Regulation 1981 (SI 1981, No. 909). London: HMSO.

Gilmer, B.vH. (1974) *Industrial and Organizational Psychology.* New York: McGraw Hill.

Goffman, E. (1959) *The Presentation of Self in Everyday Life.* New York: Doubleday Anchor.

Goffman, E. (1969) *Where the Action is.* London: Allen Lane.

Gronlund, N.E. (1970) *Stating Behavioural Objectives for Classroom Instruction.* New York: Collier-MacMillan.

Hall, E. (1959) *The Silent Language.* New York: Doubleday.

Hall, P. (1982) 'Approaching the Problem', in eds A.G. McGrew and M.J. Wilson *Decision Making. Approaches and Analysis.* Manchester: Manchester Open University Press.

Harris, T. (1967) *I'm OK – You're OK.* London: Pan.

HMSO (1989) *Children Act.* London: HMSO.

HMSO (1946) *Curtis Report.* London: HMSO.

HMSO *The Children Act 1989. Guidance and Regulations. Residential Care.* Volume 4. London: HMSO.

HMSO *The Children Act 1989. Guidance and Regulations. Independent Schools.* Volume 5. London: HMSO.

Hogben, D. (1972) 'Defining Behavioural Objectives – Some Problems and Some Dangers', *Journal of Curriculum Studies* vol. 4 no. 1, pp. 42–50.

Horney, K. (1951) *Neurosis and Human Growth.* London: Routledge & Kegan Paul.

Hunt, D.E. and Sullivan, E.V. (1974) *Between Psychology and Education.* New York: Dryden Press.

Hutchinson, S. (1991) *Perceptions of Pastoral Care in Boarding School.* Unpublished survey for M.A. dissertation, Keele University.

Independent Schools with Boarding – An Induction Framework for Social Services Inspectors, Trainers and Managers (1992) London: DOH, SSI, HMSO.

Kahan, B. (1988) 'The Physical and Mental Health of Children in Care', chapter 7 in *Child Care Research, Policy and Practice* ed. B. Kahan. Kent: Hodder & Stoughton for the Open University Press.

Kahane, R. (1977) 'Multicode Organizations: A Conceptual Framework For the Analysis of Boarding Schools', *Sociology of Education*, vol. 61, pp 211–26.

Kellmer-Pringle, M. (1980) *Fairer Future for Children.* London: MacMillan.

Kirk, K.E. (1952) *The Story of the Woodward Schools.* Abingdon Abbey Press.

Krathwohl, D.R, Bloom, B.S. and Masia, B. (1964) *Taxonomy of Educational Objectives: Affective Domain.* New York: David McKay.

Kubie, L.S. (1958) 'The Neurotic Process As the Focus of Physiological and Psychoanalytic Research', *Journal of Mental Science*, vol. 104, no. 435. (Quoted in T. Harris, 1967.)

La Fontaine, J. (1991) *Bullying: The Child's View. An Analysis of Telephone Calls to Guideline about Bullying.* Calouste Gulbenkian Foundation.

La Fontaine, J. and Morris, S. (1992) *Boarding School Line Report to the DES.* London: DES.

Laing, R.D. (1961) *Self and Others.* London: Penguin.

Laing, R.D. (1964) *Sanity, Madness and Family.* London: Tavistock/Penguin.

Lambert, R., Bullock, R. and Millham. S (1970) *A Manual to the Sociology of the School.* London: Weidenfeld & Nicholson.

Lambert, R. (1975) *A Chance of a Lifetime?: A Study of Boarding Education.* London: Weidenfeld & Nicolson.

Levy, A. and Kahan, B. (1991) *The Pindown Experience and the Protection of Children. The Report of the Staffordshire Child Care Inquiry 1990.* Staffordshire County Council.

Linton, R. (1945) *The Cultural Background to Personality.* New York: Appleton.

208

Litman, G.H. (1971) 'Climate and Motivation: An Experimental Study', in Rubin and McIntyre, D.A. Kolb, *Organizational Psychology: A Book of Readings*. London: Prentice Hall.

Lucas, N.B.C. (1975) *An Experience of Teaching*. London: Weidenfeld & Nicholson.

Maslow, A. (1943) 'A Theory of Human Motivation', *Psychological Review* vol. 50, pp. 370–96.

Mead, G. (1934) *Mind, Self and Society*. Chicago: Chicago University Press.

Measor, L. and Woods, P. (1984) *Changing Schools*. Milton Keynes: Open University Press.

Moos, R.H. (1974) *Evaluating Treatment Environments: A Social Ecological Approach*. New York: Wiley.

Moos, R.H. (1975) *Evaluating Correctional and Community Settings*. New York: Wiley.

Morgan, H.C. (1968) *Cheltenham College*. Cheltenham Society, 3.

Mulcaster, R. (1888) 'Positions', in R.H. Quick, London: Longman, pp. 222–31.

National Council of Voluntary Child Care Organizations (undated) *A Statement on Principles and Practices in Work with Children, Young People and Families*. NCVCCO.

Patterns and Outcomes (1991) *Patterns and Outcomes in Child Placement. Messages from Current Research and their Implications*. London: HMSO.

Parry, D. (1980) *Households of God. The Rule of St Benedict*.

Peters, T. (1987) *Thriving on Chaos. A Handbook for a Management Revolution*. London: MacMillan.

Porteous, J.D. (1977) *Environment and Behaviour*. Reading, Mass.: Addison-Wesley.

Porter, L.W. and Lawler, E.E. (1965) 'Properties of Organizational Structure in Relation to Job Behaviour', *Psychological Bulletin* vol. 64.

Rae, J. (1981) *The Public School Revolution*. London: Faber & Faber.

Redl, F. (1966) *When We Deal with Children*. New York: Free Press.

Report on the Revenues and Management of Certain Colleges and Schools. (Clarendon Commission), I. 1864.

Robinson, D. (1990) 'Boarding: A Need or a Challenge?' in *Boarding Education* vol. 16, BSA.

Robson, E.R. (1972) *School Architecture Report* HMSO. Presidential Speech of the RIBA, 3rd series VI (1898–9) pp. 428–32.

Rowntree, D. (1974) *Education Technology and Curriculum Development* London: Harper Row.

Rutter, M. (1991) 'Pathways from Childhood to Adult Life: The Role of Schooling', *Pastoral Care in Education*, vol. 9, no. 3.

School Life: Pupils' Views on Standards in Boarding School. (1992) R. Morgan for the Department of Health & Social Services' Inspectorate, HMSO; provisional title, to be published Autumn 1992.

Schrödinger, E. (1959) *Mind and Matter*. Cambridge: Cambridge University Press.

Slater, R. and Lipman, A. (1980) 'Towards Caring Through Design', in eds R. Walton and D. Elliott *Residential Care; A Reader in Current Theory and Practice*. London: Pergamon.

Stanley, A. (1904) *Life of Thomas Arnold*. London: John Murray.

Stewart, D. (1975) *Instruction as a Humanizing Science* vols I, II and III. Fountain Valley, California: SLATE Services.

Tiger, L. (1970) *Men in Groups*. London: Nelson.

Wagner, G. (1980) Introduction to *Residential Care: A Positive Choice,* Report of the Independent Review of Residential Care. National Institute for Social Work.

Walford, G. (1986) *Life in Public Schools.* London: Methuen.

Working Together under the Children Act 1989: A Guide to Arrangements for Inter-agency Co-operation for the Protection of Children from Abuse. (1991) London: HMSO.

Utting Report (1991) *Children in the Public Care. A Review of Residential Child Care.* London: HMSO.

Appendix I

Boarding Questionnaire

The answers you give will not identify you and they will be treated in strictest confidence. Thank you for your help.

General:
Please place a circle around the answer that applies to you or write your answer on the line provided:

1. Age: 11 12 13 14 15 16 17 18 19   2. Year: 7 8 9 10 11 L6 U6
3. Gender: male female   4. How many boarders in your house?

_____

5. Number of Years Completed in School: 0 1 2 3 4 5 6 7 8
6. Where I spent January 1st (1992): _____
                                    (town in UK or country abroad)
Accommodation:
7. The number of others I share a bedroom with: 0 1 2 3 4 5
                                               6 7 8 9 10 11 more

8. What I think the best number to share with is: _____
9. What improvements would you like to see made to your sleeping accommodation?

_____

_____

10. Are you able to shower or bath in private: Yes No
Please circle the number that most   Strongly   Strongly
nearly reflects you view: Disagree   Agree

11. I would like to shower/bath in   1   2   3   4   5   6
    private:
Telephones and telephoning:
In your last full week in school, did you:
12. Phone home?   Yes   No   13. Phone a friend?   Yes No
14. Have you ever phoned Childline or Boarding School Line Yes No
15. Is there a phone in your house you can use?   Yes No
16. Is there one outside you can use?   Yes No
17. Can you phone in the house without being overheard?   Yes No
Your feelings:
18. When you are feeling very low who do you feel happiest about turning to for comfort or advice? (circle the number nearest to your feelings)

	Least Likely		Some- times		Most Likely	
a) friend in my class or year	1	2	3	4	5	6
b) brother or sister in the school	1	2	3	4	5	6
c) phone parent(s)	1	2	3	4	5	6
d) older boy or girl	1	2	3	4	5	6
e) housemaster or housemistress	1	2	3	4	5	6
f) other house tutor or school tutor	1	2	3	4	5	6
g) head or deputy head	1	2	3	4	5	6
h) another member of staff	1	2	3	4	5	6
i) school doctor or nurse	1	2	3	4	5	6
j) chaplain	1	2	3	4	5	6
k) other						
_____	1	2	3	4	5	6

(please say who)

Bullying:
By this we mean being repeatedly hurt, mentally or physically, by another boy or girl or a group. It could include unbearable teasing or harassment − and you don't feel it is in fun.

19. Since last September I have been bullied: Yes   No
20. Since last September I have bullied someone: Yes   No
21. Since last September I have seen someone bullied: Yes   No
22. Since last September I have had some time when I
    was not spoken to by a group of my year: Yes   No
23. What clubs, hobbies or societies did you go to last week between
    Monday and Sunday?

_____

24 The things I most like about boarding here are:

_____
_____
_____

25. The things I least like about boarding here are:

_____
_____
_____

26. List three things that you think would most improve your life here:

_____

Appendix II

Design Evaluation Questionnaire

DATE ....

BUILDING NAME ....

THE SETTING

State the function, historic usage and ownership of the building

The group/individual initiating the evaluation should answer the following questions:

Respondents Name

1.   What are the five most important goals to be achieved by the evaluation of this building?

   (i) ....

   (ii) ....

   (iii)..

   (iv)...

   (v)..

2.   Which groups will use this building?

GROUP	PRIORITY RATING (1 – 10)	COMMUNICATES WITH?
....	....	....
....	....	....
....	....	....

Priority rating based on assessment of which groups have priority in affecting the goals mentioned above. 1 = low. 10 = high

Assessment to be made by the respondent.

3.   Materials and Ambient Qualities

(i)

FACTOR	EXISTING	PLANNED
Building Materials		
Building Colour		
Roofing Materials		
Roofing Colour		

(ii)   For the following components of the built environment score the building out of 10 firstly in terms of existing quality of provision and secondly for state of repair. Where appropriate the degree of privacy afforded should be taken into consideration and commented upon.

FACTOR	PROVISION STATE	COMMENT
Windows		
Doors		
Walls		
Natural Light		
Lighting External		
Lighting Internal		
Decoration		
Electrics		
Plumbing		
Heating		
Showers		
Baths		
Toilets		
Ventilation		
Drainage		
Kitchens		

Reference to be made to the Statutory Instrument 909 for specific requirements

Fittings		
Car Parking		
Access Roads		
Paths/Steps		
Waste Disposal		
Fire Exits		
Fire Alarms		
Staircases		
Telephone		
Laundry		
Store Rooms		

Hot Drink Facilities
(iii)
Room Assessment
Each room type to be identified within the building. This will vary, of
course, with the function of the building. Each room to be scored out of
10 under the headings (1 = bad, 10 = excellent)

Room	Width	Height	Light	Colour	Decor	Notes
....	....	....	....	....	....	....

(iv)
Space Assessment
Each type of space to be assessed for its quality of provision in terms of
size of space and relative location. Both are to be scored out of 10 where
1 = bad and 10 = excellent

Space	Size	Location
Personal		
Semi-personal		
Activity		
Common Room		
TV Room		
Games Room		
Library/Resources		
Quiet		
Kitchens		

(v) Assess the impact of noise (1 = low impact)
Noise
Inside Building ....
Outside Building ....
Signs − Comment on clarity, number and location
Fire
Others

THE PROXIMATE ENVIRONMENT
This element of the questionnaire attempts to assess the environment in
which the building is or will be located. Again mark the factors out of 10
(1 = lowest)

Factor	Mark	Comment
Climate		
Air Quality		
Topography		
Drainage		
Soil		
Gardens		

Natural Landscape
General Aesthetics
Building Density

THE USERS
The Users can contribute by filling in the previous sections of the
Questionnaire. However the perceptions of the Users is of particular
value. Please mark with a cross in the spaces provided how you assess
the building being evaluated.

How would you describe the .... building

	5	4	3	2	1	
impressive	( )	( )	( )	( )	( )	unimpressive
beautiful	( )	( )	( )	( )	( )	ugly
warm	( )	( )	( )	( )	( )	cold
lively	( )	( )	( )	( )	( )	static
inviting	( )	( )	( )	( )	( )	uninviting
functional	( )	( )	( )	( )	( )	not functional
like	( )	( )	( )	( )	( )	dislike
light	( )	( )	( )	( )	( )	dark
safe	( )	( )	( )	( )	( )	unsafe
effective	( )	( )	( )	( )	( )	ineffective

Index